TRUMPETING HATE

TRUMPETING HATE:

Impacts of Political Rhetoric on Minorities & America's Image

Maali W. Luqman

ISBN-13: 978-1722240530

DISCLAIMER

This book was written in the author's personal capacity. The views, thoughts, and opinions expressed in the text belong solely to the author, and not to the author's employer, any organizations, educational institutions, groups, or other individuals.

Dedication

Bismillah. In the Name of God.

This work is dedicated to my loving family and friends for their unwavering love and support that has enabled me to achieve so many of my goals and dreams. Their belief and confidence in me is the fuel that keeps me going.

I'd also like to dedicate this work to all the "Others" in America, who seem to never be accepted as American-enough. To Muslim-American brothers and sisters tackling the battles of Islamophobia during such critical times, and Native-American and African-American brethren who have fought the battles of injustice and hate in the United States since its inception, this is for you.

Finally, to all those who experience any sort of injustice, discrimination, marginalization, or hate, based on race, religion, ethnicity, or gender; you belong. When those elected to serve and lead fail at guiding their people in the direction of peace and justice for all, it is left to the people to come together, speak up and hold those in power accountable for their behaviors and actions. This work is for those who choose to unite, speak up, and stand up for what's right.

Acknowledgements

Whoever does not thank people has not thanked God.
-Prophet Muhammad
(Peace Be Upon Him)

Alhamdulillah. All Praise is to God.

I begin with the biggest thanks to God and then my mother, Samira Al-Asbahi, who worked hard and dedicated her entire life to raising my siblings and me, single-handedly, on a land foreign to her during times unfriendly to women, immigrants, Muslims, and Arabs. You are the most inspirational person I know and your resilience, perseverance, and faith inspire me every day. Words can't thank you enough for your sacrifices and only prayer for eternal bliss in this world and the next can compensate you for the lifelong efforts you've invested in my siblings and me. I'd also like to honor the memory of my father, Dr. Wijdan Luqman, who dedicated his life to the service of others. He served as Chief of Internal Medicine in the rank of Major at the Madigan Army Medical Center from 1978-1980 and continued to serve US veterans as Chief of Medicine at the Veterans Affairs Hospital in Lake City, Florida until he passed of cancer in 1999. May you rest in peace.

Next, I'd like to give a heartfelt thank you to my siblings, my brother Dr. Ali Luqman and my two sisters Widad and Samra'a Luqman. The three of you make me so proud. In everything you do, you remind me of the hardships we overcame with love, faith, loyalty, and genuine care for one another as a family to achieve successes only Mom's prayers could have made possible. A special thank you also goes to my dear friend Shayma Mustafa for believing in my work and investing time and energy in helping me complete the final step in making this book come to fruition. Thank you all and

Jazakum Allah Khair for being the pillars I needed and the answers to my prayers.

A great thanks to Professor Ousmane Kane and Professor Doug Bond at Harvard University for their guidance and priceless expertise as I completed my research for this work. I could not have accomplished such a hefty task without the direction of you both. Finally, my deepest appreciation for Attorney Albert T. Nelson for your mentorship and wisdom; you truly are a fountain of knowledge to learn from and a godsend in allowing me to blaze through trails less traveled.

Thank you all for your time, insight, and the opportunity to grow under your wings.

Preface

This book addresses the impact of President Donald Trump's negative rhetoric on minority groups in the United States and how this has a ripple effect on America's global image and international relations. This research is on the national stability of the United States following the Trump campaign with an analysis of the effects of Trump's divisive political rhetoric. It begins with a brief background on Trump's path to presidency and follows up by distinguishing between hate speech and free speech. Next, it introduces the five main minority groups most affected by Trump's political rhetoric through an exploration of their history in the United States. Following the identified minorities, the research method is introduced followed by the findings and a final conclusion on the impact of Trump's language on the studied groups and the implications this has on US global affairs.

Trump set the precedent of normalizing hate speech as president of the United States and this work analyzes the impact of language on national stability and security. The research included examines the impact of Trump's political rhetoric on women, religious, and racial minorities based on an analysis of crime statistics motivated by racial, religious, or ethnic intolerance. This research sheds light on the violence minorities have become more susceptible to since the commencement of the divisive 2016 campaign. Through an assessment of these data, the impact of Trump's political language on the stability of the diverse United States population can be observed. This was accomplished by comparing the number of reported hate crimes and violence towards minorities throughout the Trump presidential election to the reports of hate crimes and violence targeting minorities resulting from prior presidential terms. This study assesses the impacts of Trump's presidential campaign. The findings suggest that this campaign and Presidency has not only marginalized minorities within the US, but that it has also started to marginalize America from the rest of the world.

Through an evaluation of events that took place during the presidential race and into Trump's first year in office and the correlation of these events to incidents of violence and hate crimes reported by the FBI and national think tanks that targeted minorities Trump specifically rebuked in his speeches, a conclusion that Trump's political rhetoric is detrimental on the overall stability and security of the country.

The findings in this research can inform policymakers in efforts towards the regulation of hate speech. These findings can aid in distinguishing between dangerous language and acceptable political discourse in an American democracy, particularly in the cases of running political campaigns. This work also sheds light on some of the drastic consequences that can take place internationally when global affairs are provoked by increasingly harsh political rhetoric, and specifically, due to the shift from America being perceived as a world leader of change and humanitarian causes to being only American First.

CONTENTS

List of Tables

List of Figures

Definition of Terms

Anti-Semitism: a term used to depict a fear, dislike, hatred, or contempt towards Jews or those espousing the Judaic faith.

Brexit: Britain's choice to leave the European Union, which was decided by a direct popular vote and passed by just over 50%.

Black Lives Matter: the name of a movement founded in 2013 in response to the disparity in value for black lives in the United States and to bring awareness to police brutality targeting black men across the nation.

Colorism: discrimination based on the color or shade of a person's skin or proximity to whiteness.

Hispanophobia: a term used to depict a fear, dislike, hatred, or contempt towards those who originate from Latin America, more often lumped into the category of xenophobia.

Islamophobia: a term used to depict a fear, dislike, hatred, or contempt towards Muslims or those espousing the Islamic faith.

Linguistic Discrimination: the unfair treatment of people based on their use of language, including speaking a different language, a dialectal variation, or having an accent.

Misogyny: a term used to depict a dislike or contempt towards women, especially used in describing efforts to suppress women/women's rights.

People [person] of color: a term used to identify those who are not of European heritage.

Racial Battle Fatigue: the emotional, physical, and psychological toll a person of color experiences due to constant discrimination, micro-aggressions, and stereotype threat.

Stop-and-Frisk: a policy that allows police to stop anyone they suspect of criminal activity for a pat down over their clothing. Stop-and-Frisk has become a contended policy in large urban cities because of the large number of complaints of police brutality and abuses of power in large urban cities with high numbers of minorities. Many reports of discrimination by police targeting of people of color have surfaced due to Stop-and-Frisk.

Xenophobia: a term used to depict a fear, dislike, hatred, or contempt towards those who are different from oneself, especially those from different nations, ethnic backgrounds, or countries.

Introduction

America is not a blanket woven from one thread, one color, one cloth.
-Jesse Jackson

America rightly prides itself on preserving the values of liberty and equality for all. It has long been idolized as the land of the free, just, and brave for as far back as its tumultuous history takes us. The American first amendment and its protection of free speech is a constitutional right that sets America apart from most countries across the globe. From countries like North Korea to Saudi Arabia, citizens of the greater part of the world could only dream of this form of freedom of expression. Many people throughout the world would give anything for the liberty to express their thoughts and feelings freely outside the confines of their own home. Expressing dissent with government officials and political leaders offers citizens the power to challenge unjust policies and laws and take part in the progress of any nation.

Throughout history, we see how the power of language has literally changed the world. US history is rich in stories of powerful civil rights leaders, activists, and politicians that have transformed the landscape of this country through riveting speeches. Major religions across the world have inspired billions of lives based on words deemed to be revelation while tyrants and dictators have been able to rally millions of followers to carry out mass murders, ethnic cleansing, and genocides merely through their words.

Language allows people to communicate effectively. It is through words, we can understand the thoughts and feelings expressed by another. However, it also has an unseen power to move mountains of people. Because we cannot physically see the words coming out of a speaker's mouth, many are often unable to see the correlation between language and the physical world. This reality minimizes the perception regarding the impact of language use and rhetoric. However, life experience tells us otherwise. When we are motivated to transform ourselves by an inspirational speaker for instance, or we are incited to anger by the insensitive words of another, we *feel* the power of words and often are moved to act based on them. If we were able to physically see and measure the power of language using electromagnetic goggles, we would be better able to understand the art of language use as a tool to propelling forth any agenda one can conceive and be better able to comprehend its potential in changing our world.

In this book, we explore the impacts of Trump's language use on the security and stability of the United States with an emphasis on the impacts of his rhetoric on minorities in the United States. First, a brief background of the events leading to his run for presidency will be introduced, then a synopsis of the American demographic and how it has evolved, followed by the approach to the research and findings included in this work, and finally reaching a conclusion on the impacts of Trump's rhetoric on the domestic stability of the United States and the implications of his language on American global affairs.

It is assumed that protecting the right to unregulated free speech unconditionally could only bring forth good for a nation assuring that it continues to evolve with the time and demographics of its population. However, reality proves otherwise. History has taught us that words are extremely powerful and although they have the potential to influence positive progress, they can also have very dangerous impacts if expressed unchecked; exponentially so when spoken by political leaders. Hitler used political propaganda and highly demeaning language to pave the way to killing millions of Jews in Nazi Germany. Hate speech was the driving force that wiped out hundreds of thousands of Tutsis and Hutus in Rwanda's 1994 genocide. Hostile language is always the first act of violence towards others. It creates a climate conducive to physical violence through the dehumanization of its intended victims. Hate speech is often the first indicator of the intention to inflict harm upon a population.

> Hate speech is an integral part of any state-organized persecution and serves to psychologically prepare the population of a state for certain crimes planned by its leaders. It has therefore been recognized—particularly in the years since the Rwandan Genocide—that the presence of hate propaganda may indicate an impending genocide or, at least, impending violence and conflict.[1]

---

[1] Timmerman, 2008.

Although the effects of violent language are undeniable, many would argue that preserving the freedom to use any rhetoric a person chooses is essential to the preservation of American liberty. A crucial element of true freedom, the first amendment does not regulate the type of speech Americans are entitled to. So, what is the actual cost of that which is said to be free? In life, everything has its price, and the extension of one entity's liberties could come at the expense of the natural infringement of the rights of another's.

Striking the balance between one's freedom and another's security has proven to be a difficult task. Insuring that the rights of equality and stability within a nation as racially, ethnically, and religiously diverse as the American Melting Pot is even so. Accomplishing such a feat may come at the price of regulating absolute freedom of speech. For an infringement of the rights of one upon another defeats the underlying purpose of equality behind the first amendment.

The 2016 presidential election, challenged the first amendment's confines of the exercise of free speech. With Donald Trump extending his exercise of free speech to spread false stereotypes and incite violence towards minority groups, people began to question the boundaries of free speech. Preserving the right that allows public statements that target entire populations of one's own citizens, comments that stir up civil strife or threaten a nation's stability and its international relations seemed to defy the unspoken limits of free speech. The inception of the 2016 presidential campaign had the world over questioning what exactly American free speech is and how far its umbrella will stretch to protect hate driven rhetoric that poses serious threats to the security of groups of its citizens and the rest of the world.

Hate Speech vs. Free Speech:
Where do we draw the line?

Let us not seek to satisfy our thirst for freedom by drinking from the cup of bitterness and hatred.
-Martin Luther King Jr.

The American First Amendment has paved the way to justice and equality for Americans for centuries. It is a golden rule that protects all citizens from the abuse of power by the government and allows them to express themselves without fear of persecution or harm. The protection of free speech is essential to progress in any organization, society, or government and this right, promised to all American citizens, has been protected for as far back as it dates. However, when does the protection of this right become a disservice to the American people? As all things are in this world, if this liberty is not regulated it can surely be abused and taken to an extreme. So, at what point should the American people label free speech as hate speech? Is there a barometer of language use that we can put to the test of questionable rhetoric that can redefine what constitutes free speech as opposed to hate speech? And if so, can we outlaw divisive language that fits the definition?

The 2016 presidential campaign definitely brought these questions to the limelight of political and legal discussions regarding the rights to free speech. In June 2017, the Supreme court affirmed that any legal regulations of free speech would pose a threat to the freedom of it and consequently make legal regulation of speech unconstitutional.[2] However, the spike in reports of hate crimes that swept the nation with the racist rhetoric employed by Donald Trump during his campaign and into his Presidency lead us to question the impacts of unregulated speech on the well-being of a nation.

Hate speech is driven by malicious intent while other forms of language are inspired by different motives. Hate speech is not only dangerous to those it is directed at, it is also detrimental to the well-being of those inspired by it. Murrow and Murrow's research on the relationship between neurology, dehumanization, and human rights discusses the neurological processes that occur when humans engage in the dehumanization of others.[3] With professional backgrounds in Law and Neurology, their research delves into discussions pertaining to mirror neurons, those related to empathy and language in the human brain, and how dehumanization is conditioned in the brain. Roginsky and Tsesis make a connection between Murrow and Murrow's hypothesis by suggesting that dehumanization plays the first step in carrying out violence on others.[4] To dehumanize others is to strip them of the qualities that allow them to be perceived as human, disrupting our ability to empathize, identify with their experiences, or see them as other people. Hate speech is the first

---

[2] Volokh, 2017.

[3] Murrow & Murrow, 2015.

[4] Roginsky & Tsesis, 2016.

act of violent aggression towards those hearing it as well as those it targets. It destroys the mirror neuron's ability to experience empathy for those it directs its hate to, dehumanizing the target, while blinding the hater's mind of its natural rationale; making the one inspired by the language capable of carrying out acts of violence. With these neurons turned off, empathy is not felt for others. The connection between these neurons and language is what transforms hate speech into physical violence. The moment that hate-inspired rhetoric is received by the brain is the first act of violence towards the one receiving it. Either their empathetic abilities are harmed through the suppression of the natural human reaction to mirror the feelings of others or the violent language triggers them to feel the same pain as the one the hate was intended to harm. Those that allow that violence to penetrate their minds without rejecting it, are robbed of their human instinct to empathize. This violates their human nature in an unseen way, making all those hearing that rhetoric the first victims of hate speech. If that language is accepted and internalized, it translates into the justified dehumanization of others, which enables aggressors to lash out on those they perceive as less human. This is the first step towards violations of human rights and poses a major threat to the security of a nation and its people. Lakoff, a retired distinguished Professor of cognitive science and linguistics at the University of California and Director of the Center for the Neural Mind & Society, echoes these findings.

> All thought is carried out by neural circuitry — it
> does not float in air. Language neurally activates

thought. Language can thus change brains, both for the better and the worse. Hate speech changes the brains of those hated for the worse, creating toxic stress, fear and distrust — all physical, all in one's neural circuitry active every day. This internal harm can be even more severe than an attack with a fist. It imposes on the freedom to think and therefore act free of fear, threats, and distrust. It imposes on one's ability to think and act like a fully free citizen for a long time. That's why hate speech imposes on the freedom of those targeted by the hate. Since being free in a free society requires not imposing on the freedom of others, hate speech does not fall under the category of free speech. Hate speech can also change the brains of those with mild prejudice, moving it towards hate and threatening action. When hate is physically in your brain, then you think hate and feel hate, you are moved to act to carry out what you physically, in your neural system, think and feel. That is why hate speech is not "mere" speech. And since it imposes on the freedom of others, it is not an instance of freedom. The long–term, often crippling physical effects of hate speech on the neural systems of those hated does not have status in law, since our neural systems do not have status in our legal system — at least not yet. This is a gap between the law and the truth.[5]

In history, we see that all major acts of genocide and war began with this step of the dehumanization of people.

> Hate speakers rely on dehumanizing images to justify exclusion, discrimination, and, in genocidal cases, elimination of identifiable groups. Dehumanization can be both an attack on the target's dignity and a justification for harmful actions. Statements dehumanizing hated groups often influence the commission of discriminatory conduct. The critical role of rhetoric in motivating nefarious action is evident in the histories of genocides in Germany, Turkey, Sudan, and Rwanda. In all of these countries, the official spread of malignant and distorted images of the other (Jews, Armenians, Darfuris, and Tutsis, respectively) made it easy to bring the hated groups into disrepute with the population and cleared the way to their mass killing and divestment of property.[6]

That is why it is imperative to develop a critical distinction between free speech and hate speech and take a solid

---

[5] Lakoff, 2017.
[6] Roginsky & Tsesis, 2016.

stance against the latter. A good barometer to measure where to draw the line between the two would be in reference to our physiological reactions to each. Free speech does not harm the brain while hate speech initiates unnatural neurological responses in our brains such as the suppression of mirrored neurons.

In the case of Donald Trump, the rhetoric he employed demonstrates an evident lack of empathy or humanization towards groups such as, but not limited to, African-Americans, Hispanics, Women, Muslims, and Immigrants. Given a platform to amplify these sentiments is poisonous to the minds of all those exposed to this rhetoric. Furthermore, a suppression of natural brain activity reduces the brain's ability to function at an optimal human level. So consequently, there is truth to the notion that hate diminishes from one's cognitive performance and intellectual capacity - a possible factor contributing to the president's limited vocabulary evident during his public addresses and discourse.

Background

You're not supposed to be so blind with patriotism that you can't face reality.
Wrong is wrong, no matter who does it or says it.
-Malcolm X

On June 16, 2015 news releases across the country flooded with reports of Donald Trump's bid for United States Presidency. After 8 years of Barack Hussein Obama's leadership, the first African-American president with Muslim lineage,[7] Trump felt inclined to commence his presidential campaign stating that the country needed somebody that could make America great again, and expressed that he would take on the task.[8] Although Trump had no background in politics, law, or international affairs, he had the wealth to fund his own campaigning and the fame and following through his celebrity status to drive it forward. His billionaire prestige and popularity gave him the head start he needed to jump right into the run for United States Presidency.

Throughout his campaign, Trump repeatedly called on his supporters to use violence, saying that protesters should be taken out on stretchers, he would foot any legal bills should they arise from such violence, and that he, when met with a protester,

---

[7] Holan, 2010.

[8] DelReal, 2015.

would personally like to have "punched him in the face."[9] When a black man was attacked at one of his rallies for protesting for the *Black Lives Matter* movement,[10] Trump justified the attack, by tweeting that the protester "should have been roughed up."[11] The list of violent incidents during Trump's campaign goes on to include the bombing of a mosque in Canada,[12] a Sikh man being shot in 2016 in Seattle having been mistaken for a Muslim,[13] and two men being stabbed to death by a white nationalist as they defended a Muslim girl wearing a head scarf on a train in Portland from a barrage of insults by a nationalist, who demanded she go back to Saudi Arabia.[14] All these incidents, and plenty more occurring with the fervor of Trump's political rhetoric throughout his bid for presidency and into his term in office.

---

[9] O'Connor & Marans, February 29, 2016.

[10] Black Lives Matter: the name of a movement founded in 2013 in response to the disparity in value for black lives in the United States and to bring awareness to police brutality targeting black men across the nation.

[11] O'Connor & Marans, February 29, 2016.

[12] Dougherty, January 31, 2017.

[13] Moshtaghian, Wu, & Cullinane, March 6, 2017.

[14] CNN Wire, May 30, 2017.

The Illustrious American Identity

We don't need a melting pot in this country, folks. We need a salad bowl. In a salad bowl, you put in the different things. You want the vegetables-the lettuce, the cucumbers, the onions, the green peppers-to maintain their identity. You appreciate differences.
-Jane Elliot

The United States of America is a nation built upon diversity. It is a nation that promises people of all ethnicities, religions, socioeconomic status, and background equality and the opportunity at reaching the heights of success and prosperity. Because of this promise, many people from all across the globe have bought into this American dream and immigrated to the country either to flee persecution or in pursuit of an opportunity at a better life. As far back as the history of the United States dates, we see that immigration has been one of the central traits of the nation. Scholars and Researchers unanimously concur on this note. "From the founding days of the republic to present times, international migration has been the defining attribute of American society."[15] If this feature of American demographics distinguishes it from most other nations across the globe, why has immigration become such an issue of great dissent in modern American politics and why do we see such a magnitude of social fragmentation across the United

---

[15] Hirschman, Kasinitz, & Dewind, 1999, 1.

States even in this modern day and age? To better understand the demographic of modern-day America and the perceived threats associated with immigration, let's briefly revisit America's immigration history.

A Brief History of US Demographics

We may have all come on different ships, but we're in the same boat now.
–Martin Luther King Jr.

America's foundation was based on immigrant populations building a new life, oceans away from their native lands. With the exception of Native Americans, who now comprise only a minute segment of today's American population, all other citizens today are either immigrants, descendants of immigrants, or descendants of Africans brought to the America's forcefully through slavery.

In 1492 Europeans stumbled upon the Americas en route to the Near East and began colonization of the land, killing off the majority of its indigenous population with the establishment of the new nation. In 1776 the United States of America was founded, on the principles of equality and liberty mentioned above. Although the founding fathers were of European descent, they built the nation off the backs of enslaved Africans, a large proportion who were Muslim.[16] Within 85 years, the principles enshrined in the constitution were challenged and civil war across the young nation erupted. In January of 1863, the Emancipation Proclamation granted slaves in the rebellious territories their freedom and led the United States one step in the

---

[16] Derosa, 2016.

direction of its current demography.[17] Although the proclamation only freed few slaves, it affirmed that the US civil war had evolved into a war to end slavery.

As the Age of Mass Migration[18] swept the nation and no restrictions on international migration initially established, waves of immigrants from all over the world filled the labor force, again transforming the national population.

> America's door was essentially open to all immigrants willing and able to come. It was not until 1917 that the U.S. Congress took measures to restrict immigration with literacy requirements and an expanded prohibition of Asian immigration. A few years later, the Quota Law of 1921 imposed numerical restrictions for the first time on immigration from non-Western Hemisphere countries and then these quotas were reduced in 1924. The impact was dramatic.[19]

---

[17] Schwartz, 2015.

[18] Carter & Sutch, 2006, 5.

[19] Carter & Sutch, 2006, 5.

Due to unregulated immigration policies and an appetite for growth, the country's immigrant population continued to transform. Within just a few generations, the growing nation's racial and cultural image became a weave of diverse threads.

Today's number of recent immigrants is rapidly growing. *The Handbook of International Migration* tells us that "[m]ore than 50 million Americans – one-fifth of the total population – are immigrants or the children of immigrants."[20] This statistic is only representative of new generations of immigrants. With a nation founded on centuries of the immigration of people from all across the globe, it is inconceivable to define such a country with a homogeneous race, culture, or uniform identity. This is exactly what makes America so exceptional; its strength through it's diversity, promise for equal opportunity, and evolution of a global identity.

> It is hard to imagine any part of American history or popular culture that has not been touched by immigration. The Statue of Liberty is perhaps the most widely understood cultural icon of American society, both at home and abroad...The notion that almost any person from anywhere can

---

[20] Hirschman, Kasinitz, & Dewind, 1999, 1.

"make it in America" has had a powerful impact on the image of America abroad and at home.[21]

However, due to this unique American trait and an evolving image of an American, many Americans with early European ancestry feel that their idea of an American identity is being threatened by an influx of immigrants. They fail to realize that a distinguished characteristic of what defines an American is that it is based on an evolving, malleable culture that has no uniform color or face. This perceived threat to an identity that is not physically defined is what drives much of the political discussion surrounding immigration policies as well as the struggles for social equality battled by minority communities in America. "The debates over immigration law are part of the larger question of national identity that influences almost every aspect of political, social, and cultural life."[22]

So, if America is truly just a melting pot of cultures or a salad bowl of races, how does that look? If equal opportunity is promised to all, does a particular image drive the policies and social privileges that favor certain segments of the American public than others? Why are some opportunities more accessible to Americans that fit that certain envisioned image of who an American is and who created that image to begin with? Finally,

---

[21] Hirschman, Kasinitz, & Dewind, 1999, 1.

[22] Hirschman, Kasinitz, & Dewind, 1999, 8.

how does the American dream truly manifest itself in reality and who is getting marginalized? A brief exploration of the history of several minority groups and the issues they face along with the stigmas they battle today reveal the answers to these pressing questions. Let's begin by taking a close look at the history of our largest racial minority group, African-Americans, in the United States.

African-Americans

In diversity there is beauty and there is strength.
-Maya Angelou

According to the 2010 United States Census, African-Americans account for 12.6% of the U.S. population.[23] African-Americans have a deep and painful history in the United States. There is a small percentage of African immigrants that came to the land freely and do not share the American history of slavery and the struggle for human and civil rights that most African-Americans do. A greater number of African-Americans in the United States are descendants of slavery, brought across the Atlantic in bondage on slave ships and enslaved by white European-Americans. The chapter of this period in world history is grim and carries a huge burden of collective guilt on the world for all the suffering endured by millions of Africans that fell victim to this atrocity. The United States is especially admonished for this grave racial injustice because the nation was established through the blood, sweat, and tears of this oppressed group of people, and the consequences of this era of injustice remain until today.

People of African descent have a history that dates back further than the 16th century. Estimates suggest that roughly 14,650,000 African slaves were shipped across the Atlantic to

---

[23] US Census, 2010.

the New World between the 16th and 19th century alone.[24] After the liberation of slaves in the United States, black people in the US continued to be enslaved through a system of oppression and structural racism that hindered them from experiencing the same levels of equality as their white counterparts. These include Jim Crow legislation, social restrictions, and institutional barriers. With remnants of white supremacy alive and widespread, African-Americans still continue to face institutionalized and cultural racism from achieving true freedom and equality alongside their fellow white Americans. Today, the African-American minority battles structural and cultural violence, gross misrepresentation in the media that fuels policies and brutal treatment towards them, and racism of all forms in every aspect of their day to day lives.

Policies including "Stop and Frisk"[25] targeting black people and diasporas of people of color across the country, agendas that perpetuate police brutality and mass incarceration, voter suppression tactics targeting black communities, and little to no sentencing for law enforcement taking innocent black lives during traffic stops are all symptoms of the inherited anti-black

---

[24] Curtin, 1972, 5.

[25] Elkins, 2015.

racism that continues to plague the United States until today. An analysis of FBI data conducted by Dana Lind with VOX news revealed that police in the US take the lives of black people and other people of color[26] at disproportionate rates to whites throughout the country.

> Black people accounted for 31 percent of police killing victims in 2012, even though they made up just 13 percent of the US population…Racial minorities made up about 37.4 percent of the general population in the US…but they made up 62.7 percent of unarmed people killed by police.[27]

On July 8, 2016, following the deaths of Philando Castile and Alton Sterling by police, Ricardo A. Sunga III (Human rights expert and Chair of the United Nations Working Group of Experts on People of African Descent) addressed the severity of police brutality in the US towards African-American men. He issued a statement addressing the link between structural racism and the alarming regularity of black lives being lost during basic traffic stops or reports to 911 calls in the US.

---

[26] People [person] of color: a term used to identify those who are not of European heritage.

[27] Lopez, November 14, 2018.

The Working Group is outraged and strongly condemns the new police killings of two African-American men…Excessive use of force by the police against African Americans in the United States is a regular occurrence. African Americans are reportedly shot at more than twice the rate of white people…The Working Group is monitoring the situation and has repeatedly expressed its concern to the United States Government about police killings of African Americans and called for justice. The Working Group is convinced that the root of the problem lies in the lack of accountability for perpetrators of such killings despite the evidence…The killings also demonstrate a high level of structural and institutional racism. The United States is far from recognizing the same rights for all its citizens. Existing measures to address racist crimes motivated by prejudice are insufficient and have failed to stop the killings.[28]

Philando Castile and Alton Sterling were just two of many black lives lost due to reactionary responses by law enforcement. Philando Castile, was pulled over for a broken tail light with his girlfriend and her 4-year old daughter in the car on July 6, 2016

---

[28] United Nations Office of High Commissioner of Human Rights, July, 6, 2018.

in Falcon Heights, Minnesota. He informed police he was carrying a firearm and was shot during the traffic stop as he reached for his wallet (based on the statement of his girlfriend and video footage), while the officer assumed he was reaching for a gun.[29]

Alton Sterling was shot just the day before in Baton Rouge, Lousiana, as officers reported to a 911 call stating that Sterling was selling CDs outside a convenience store and that he had drew out a gun. Upon their arrival, Sterling did not have a gun drawn and was shot as they attempted to restrain him, reporting they thought he too was reaching for one in his pocket. Witnesses state that at no point was a gun visible, however, Sterling was still killed during the scuffle.[30] Similar cases have been reported throughout the country with little to no accountability for hasty reactions taken by law enforcement. This is an indicator of bias, whether implicit or explicit, held by officers towards men of color that surfaces during intense situations. This lends itself back to insufficient training of our

---

[29] Croft, CNN, June 21, 2017.

[30] Almasy, Yan, Lynch, & Levenson, CNN, June 27, 2017. Berlinger, Valencia, & Almasy, CNN, July 8, 2016.

law enforcement, misrepresentations of data and internalized stereotypes, and an indicator of institutionalized racism.

Furthermore, data surrounding the number of arrests made in relation to the percent of actual criminal activity reveal the disparity in racial inequity when it comes to law enforcement in the US. Based on a 2013 national survey conducted on illicit drug use and health by the U.S Department of Health and Human Services, 9.5% of users were white while 10.5% were black.[31] However, according to FBI crime reports and the US Census, there were only 332 drug-related arrests of white perpetrators in contrast to 879 black arrests per 100,000.[32] This, not including a breakdown of which non-black ethnic minorities were included for the count of whites. With racial bias affecting how the laws are enforced, there is a larger proportion of black men and women in US prisons than whites. According to a study conducted by the NAACP in 2014, African-Americans comprised of 34% of those in correctional facilities. Their incarceration rate is over 5 times that of whites, with black women being twice as likely to be locked up than white women. Along with Hispanics, African-Americans made

----

[31] Lopez, November 14, 2018 & U.S. Department of Health and Human Services, 2013.

[32] Lopez, November 14, 2018.

up 56% of the US prison population in 2015. These two minorities combined, equate to only about 32% of the general US population.[33]

With a racist lens of observation, these statistics may lead one to believe that these minorities are inherently more violent and crime prone. However, the disparity we witnessed in the data regarding whites that are involved in similar criminal activity yet are not proportionally convicted for those crimes actually reveals the racial bias clouding the lens of the interpretation of this data. These numbers demonstrate that there is evident discrimination in the enforcement of the same laws for those who identify as black or as people of color. Economic inequities, environmental injustices, and lack of equal educational and professional opportunities affecting these minorities due to racial biases and discrimination also feed into the increase of crime in marginalized communities. This in turn increases police surveillance of these populations, along with higher reports of police brutality, and contributes to higher incarceration rates; not allowing for the wounds ensuing from covert and institutionalized racism to heal. This only perpetuates the cycle of injustice marginalizing people of color.

In 1989, five young African-American and Latino teenage boys were wrongfully convicted of brutally raping and

---

[33] NAACP, 2018.

beating a female jogger in New York City. The story of the Central Park Five revealed the effects of institutionalized racism and the impacts of race-baiting in New York City which led to the wrongful conviction of five innocent youth. [34] Although there were clear discrepancies in the testimonies of the young men and lack of sufficient evidence pointing towards their association in the crime, the five teenagers were arrested, relentlessly interrogated, and then imprisoned due to faulty confessions coerced by fear. The age of these boys was not adequality taken into account when their testimonies were taken, yet their statements lead to their guilty verdicts despite the contradictions in each of their recounts of what had occurred the night of the crime. Donald Trump, leading business tycoon at that time, lead efforts employing divisive rhetoric, pushing for the death penalty for these black and brown youth. It was not until 2002 when the boys had already served significant prison time, that Matias Reyes, a serial rapist, came out with his solid confession, including specific details about the incident, and DNA evidence linking him to the crime. Even with the detailed confession which perfectly aligned with specific evidence at the site of the crime, along with the settlement in 2014 issued by the city that further exonerated these young men, Trump persisted

---

[34] Sundance Selects, WETA, Florentine Films, PBS, The Central Park Five Film Project, 2012.

with indications that they remain guilty.[35] This incident, the 1973 lawsuit carried out by the Justice Department against Donald Trump, his father, and the Trump company for violating the Fair Housing Act of 1968 towards people of color,[36] along with other reports of Trump's racially discriminating practices shed light on Trump's sentiments towards African-Americans and people of color prior to his bid for presidency.

As Trump began his political run, he brought much of these inherited biases and racist views on his campaign trail and many more. The Black minority experienced a 2016 political campaign unfriendly to them. Besides self-proclaiming himself to be the man who started the Birther Movement, Donald Trump refused to acknowledge that President Barack Obama was indeed a citizen until September 2016. He also refused to indicate that he no longer believed Obama was a Muslim, implying that being Muslim was un-American. Trump also refused to condemn David Duke, a former KKK leader at least three times during a live CNN Interview with Jake Tapper.[37] As he took office he responded to racial justice issues with extreme

---

[35] Fisher, August 16, 2017. Hutchinson, October 8, 2017. Laughland, February 17, 2016. Sarlin, October 7, 2016.

[36] United States District Court for the Eastern District of New York, 1975.

[37] Collinson & Diamond, September 16, 2016.

leniency towards violent white nationals and severe intensity towards peacefully protesting black athletes. Trump's response to the Charlottesville murder that ensued due to protests pertaining to the removal of controversial confederate statues trivialized the magnitude of the crime. White supremacist, Neo-Nazi James Alex Fields Jr. rammed his vehicle at full speed into a crowd of counter protestors injuring 19 people and killing one.[38] Other reports of violence erupting during this protest were also reported.

Trump's presidential address was directing equal blame for the bloodshed on both parties and dismissing the alt-right's accountability for initiating such a violent event. Rather than condemning the death of an innocent protestor in support of racial equality, President Trump instead described the alt-right protesters as including "very fine people," and justifying the actions carried out by the alt-right through implications that they were provoked to carry out such acts of violence by the opposing group. In strike contrast, the president had no hesitation reproaching numbers of black athletes who peacefully demonstrated disapproval of racial injustice at sports events. He expressed a blatant pre-dispositioned response towards black NFL players taking a knee during the national anthem in silent

---

[38] Almasy, S., Hanna, J., Hartung, K., Sayers, D. & CNN, August 13, 2017.

protest towards police brutality targeting people of color. Although these athletes committed no crime by merely exercising their right to protest, Trump unleashed an infuriated and enraged response referring to the athletes in derogatory terms on public television and suggesting they be fired for this exercise of free speech.[39] He referred to all star athletes such as San Francisco 49ers quarterback Colin Kaepernick as "sons of bitches" for expressing their dissension with the widespread reports of police brutality towards black Americans throughout the country. This peaceful effort to bring light to this serious national issue by the athletes was portrayed as an unpatriotic act of disrespect rather than a noble stance against discriminatory and racists acts of violence that were recklessly taking countless lives of innocent black Americans throughout the country. In striking contrast, the white nationalists in Charlottesville violated many laws, broke out in riots of violence, and their actions resulted in murder and domestic terrorism. However, Trump's stance towards the white supremacists was dismissive due to the race of the protestors.[40] His obsessive criticism of the first black president or black athletes standing for social justice in comparison to his complacent approval towards violent white nationalist reveals the algorithm to Trump's values system towards equality and justice for Americans. The disparity in the

---

[39] Tatum, September 23, 2017.

[40] Brownstein, September 25, 2017.

president's responses to each event that took place reveals Trump's methods of determining right and wrong as president of the United States and leader of the free world. It is evident that race played a role in determining which actions Trump perceived as more heinous. Leadership that bases its value system on this type of racial inequality paves the way for hate crimes, violence, and injustice towards anyone other than white nationalists.

Hispanics

*Preservation of one's own culture does not require contempt or disrespect for
other cultures.*
-Cesar Chavez

Latino-Americans are descendants of Spanish speaking
territories and states including Mexico, Cuba, Puerto Rico, and
Spain. They are also commonly referred to as Hispanic-
Americans. At 16.3% of total United States population,[41]
Hispanic-Americans are the second largest ethnic minority
group in the United States following those who identify as
white. Whites, however, also include different unspecified non-
Hispanic sub-groups such as Arabs in this census. This indicates
that Anglo-American whites, actually comprise a smaller
percentage of US population than that which is indicated in the
2010 US Census.

Hispanic-Americans have been in the United States since
as far back as the land has had its earliest European explorers.
With early Spanish explorers reaching all the way to the West
coast, Hispanic-Americans have a deep-rooted history on
American land. Although a significant proportion of this
American minority can trace themselves back to the foundation
of the nation, a large fragment of the Hispanic-American

---

[41] US Census, 2010.

population today are recent immigrants from the neighboring country Mexico. Mexican Latinos comprise over half of all Hispanic-Americans.[42] With a high demand for seasonal farm labor along the western United States, many Mexicans were able to find work in these western states and chose to migrate.

Although the abundance of low wage labor helped farmers sustain their industry, the influx of new Mexican immigrants posed a threat to the pre-existing culture in the region, instigating tensions between white and Hispanic Americans and propelling anti-Mexican sentiments by white Americans across the US.

Donald Trump made headlines when he commenced his campaign with a call to deport Mexicans, stating "When Mexico sends its people, they're not sending their best...They're bringing drugs; They're bringing crime; They're rapists, and some, I assume, are good people."[43] The call was heard, and many Americans, resentful of economic disparity, gladly accepted that their economic strife was a result of illegal immigration and joined in on his chants to build a border wall along the southern US border, with the promise of Mexico footing the bill. Although Trump offered no material plans as to how he intended to accomplish this outlandish guarantee of protecting the United States from the unsubstantiated infiltration of criminals from the Mexican border, scapegoaters quickly

---

[42] Gutrel, 2008.

[43] Washington Post Staffer, June 16, 2015.

cheered him on. This heated assertion began paving the path to normalizing racist rhetoric and marginalizing a significant population of the American people.

As Trump's campaign continued unchecked and his divisive demeanor defended and applauded, Trump was emboldened by his followers and reciprocated their support by promising to protect those who acted out in violence towards those he opposed. When his supporters beat up a Hispanic homeless man, one saying to police, "Donald Trump was right- all these illegals need to be deported," rather than denouncing their actions, Trump responded with praise that his followers (these men) were passionate and loved this country.[44] To further his prejudice claims towards Mexicans, Trump went on to attack the veracity of an esteemed United States Federal Judge. In response to a judicial ruling against his failed University, Trump accused United Stated District Judge Gonzalo Curiel of Mexican descent of an inability to be impartial as a direct result of his Mexican heritage. "He's a Mexican. We're building a wall between here and Mexico. The answer is, he is giving us very unfair rulings-rulings that people can't even believe."[45] The reality that a presidential candidate would publicly insult the integrity of an honorable Judge by employing such racist statements was responded to with shock.

---

[44] O'Connor & Marans, February 29, 2016.

[45] Washington Post Staffer, June 16, 2015.

Outcries against Trump's speech were heard immediately following each statement. But Mexicans were not alone.

Women

Our glorious diversity – our diversities of faiths and colors and creeds – that is not a threat to who we are, it makes us who we are.
-Michelle Obama

The 2010 United States census suggests that women make up 51% of the national population.[46] Although this group is not identified as a minority due to their size, they are grouped alongside minorities impacted by Trump's political rhetoric in this book because they remain marginalized in positions of power, government, and other aspects of American society. American women are equally as racially and ethnically diverse as the entire US demographic. Although women in the United States have set precedent for other women throughout the globe in certain aspects, the struggle to get women to the point they have reached in America today was no easy task, and they still lag behind men in government representation, pay, access to equitable opportunities at professional advancement, and other gender related social issues. They suffer from gender bias in their personal, social, and professional lives and experience less

---

[46] Annual Estimates of the Resident Population for Selected Age Groups by Sex for the United States, States, Counties and Puerto Rico Commonwealth and Municipios: April 1, 2010 to July 1, 2016 Source: U.S. Census Bureau, Population Division Release Date: June 2017.

financial and professional attainability than men. New research by Harvard Business School's assistant professor Mark Egan revealed that "Women caught in misconduct were 20 percent more likely to be fired and 30 percent less likely to find new employment in the financial services industry."[47] This study concluded that there was evident gender bias towards women in this male-dominated, high paying professional field. Along with reports of women-dominated careers being grossly underpaid including professions such as education and nursing, various low-wage female-dominated occupations lack benefits and have poor working conditions.[48] Women suffer gender inequality in securing a fair livelihood. The Institute for Women's Policy Research found that

> Women's concentration in occupations and sectors with relatively low pay is a major factor behind the gender wage gap (Blau and Kahn 2016). Women have lower earnings both because the occupations that mainly employ women tend to have lower earning than occupations that mainly employ men (for any worker in that occupation, whether they are men or women) and because women face sex discrimination (they earn less than men when they work in the same

---

[47] Blanding, December 18, 2018.

[48] Institute for Women's Policy Research, 2016.

occupation; Hegewisch and Hartmann 2014).
This is especially true for women of color, who
face additional discrimination because of their
racial or ethnic identity (Wilson 2016).[49]

Women experience pay inequality, earning approximately only
79 percent of the median wage of what men earn based on data
available until 2014.[50] They have less access to full-time work
and better employment opportunities, although 15% are single
mothers and in need of better paying jobs.[51] Women also
comprise 55.2% of college students although men in the United
States continue to earn significantly more than women with
equal or similar qualifications.[52] Furthermore, sexual harassment
on the job is a real threat for many women in all occupations,
but increasingly so in low-wage jobs.

> For women working in occupations where tips
> make up a large part of earnings, the pressure to
> act friendly, if not sexualized, is particularly
> strong; and the threat of losing tips makes it even
> harder to challenge harassment on the job,

---

[49] Institute for Women's Policy Research, 2016.

[50] United States Congress, 2016.

[51] Institute for Women's Policy Research, 2016.

[52] US Census, 2016.

whether such harassment is sexual, racial, or age-related. Sexual harassment is particularly common in restaurants, where employers may see it in their interest not to censure customers who behave inappropriately towards their staff despite legal prohibitions on employers knowingly permitting third-party/customer harassment.[53]

These studies in regard to women and employment alone reveal the great disparity between male and female inequity in the US.

Women in America have been fighting for equal rights for centuries. The beginning of the women suffrage movement dates back to 1848 but efforts towards women's equal rights can be traced back all the way to 1807.[54] The marginalization of this group is evident in their underrepresentation in positions of leadership and politics and like other groups, made them easy targets for Trump's hate speech during his 2016 presidential campaign.

---

[53] Institute for Women's Policy Research, 2016.

[54] Fawcett, 1912, 8.

According to the Center for American Women and Politics,

> In 2017, 105 (78D, 27R) women h[e]ld seats in the United States Congress, comprising 19.6% of the 535 members; 21 women (21%) serve[d] in the United States Senate, and 84 women (19.3%) serve[d] in the United States House of Representatives.[55]

That's a significant underrepresentation of women in United States government. Hilary Clinton was the first female presidential candidate to reach the primaries. She faced much harsh sexist criticism and attacks from adversary Donald Trump and his followers during her run for presidency.

Women were repeatedly objectified and victimized by Trump during his presidential Campaign. Trump was unrelenting on vocal females, often attacking them personally or insulting them based on their physical appearance. Trump demeaned women publicly since 2015, with amplified rage towards his female opponents or those who he felt were attacking him. Starting with suggestions that Carly Fiorina, his Republican primary opponent, could not attain votes because of her looks, Trump shamelessly continued fueling his campaign by attacking the personal life of his primary opponent Hillary

---

[55] Center for American Women and Politics, 2017.

Clinton, the Democratic presidential candidate. Trump claimed Clinton was to blame for her husband's past infidelity in reference to the Monica Lewinsky scandal. He asserted that Mrs. Clinton lacked the ability to fulfill her role as a wife by stating she could not satisfy her husband and enabled him to cheat. Trump continued his run for presidency ignorantly addressing highly sensitive policy issues concerning women's rights using an equally sexist tone and insular approach to evaluating national policies. He blatantly stated that women who get abortions should face criminal punishment with a complete disregard for the pertinent discussions surrounding this critical issue. Trump's sexist rhetoric goes on to him calling journalist Megyn Kelley a bimbo and reigniting a feud with former Miss America, Alicia Machado, again reiterating that she "gained a massive amount of weight." He then continued by tweeting that Machado had a sex tape.[56] He built momentum by fueling his campaign through language he referred to as mere "locker-room talk" rather than addressing real issues with solid arguments and operative politically relevant dialogue. This vile campaign delivered him his Presidency, taking him to the most powerful leadership role in the world, albeit based on faulty and divisive foundations.

---

[56] Cohen, January 20, 2017.

Jews

Thou shalt love thy neighbour as thyself.
-Leviticus 19:18

It is believed that along with Muslims and Christians, some Jews accompanied Columbus when he sailed to America.[57] The Jewish American demographic also has deep roots in American colonial history. The Jewish community grew in number in the 1800s as immigration to the United States grew. Many German Jews fleeing the Holocaust found refuge in the United States in the early to mid 1900s. They began growing their communities by building places of worship and small businesses, specifically along the United States east coast. Many Jews were politically engaged, and pursued higher education, climbing the American social ladder of success rapidly. Today, Jewish Americans are 3% of the United States population, concentrated in diasporas within urban cities along the east coast.[58]

With antisemitism targeting many people of the Jewish faith, this minority has faced its share of struggles. Along with other marginalized communities, Jews were objects of discrimination throughout American history.

---

[57] Peters, 1905.

[58] Pew Research Center, 2015 & Jewish Virtual Library, 2017.

Is the American milieu ready to fuel a poisonous political climate, where demonizing an entire ethnic or religious community is seen as acceptable? America's history clearly speaks to severe discrimination against other groups, such as African Americans, Hispanics, women, gays and lesbians, and many others. But perhaps no community in the West has been the victim of millennia-long persecution and "othering" campaigns as have the Jews. [59]

Although there has been a drastic shift of prejudicial focus since the events that took place September 11, 2001, persecution for religious identity is nothing new to United States hate trends.

Jews saw many attacks and stereotypes hurled their way during the Trump presidential campaign as well. While speaking to the Republican Jewish Coalition in a December 2015 fundraiser, Trump repeatedly made comments regarding Jews and money. In July 2016, Trump retweeted a picture of Hillary on a magazine cover from a white supremacist/neo-Nazi forum, with money in the background, and the Star of David in front, insisting that it was a harmless figure that he himself had created. Upon taking office, Trump refused, on multiple occasions, to denounce the anti-Semitic violence that was

---

[59] Aslan & Tapper, 2011.

making national headlines. Then as a final blow, while speaking at the Holocaust Memorial on Holocaust Remembrance Day, he did not mention Jews as being the main targets of the Holocaust altogether.[60] Shortly, thereafter, a forthcoming surge in desecration of Jewish synagogues and bomb threats seized Jewish communities nationwide.

Trump's attitudes towards Jews demonstrate his xenophobic views regarding this group of people domestically. However, with his hate towards Muslims evidently stronger, Trump made the divisive decision to recognize Jerusalem as Israel's capital on December 6, 2017.[61] This controversial decision shook the world, jeopardizing nearly half a century of peace talks and undermining one of the central components of the two-state solution that had long been discussed. This bold and reckless move sparked protests and violence to erupt in Jerusalem and earned the condemnation of 128 nations in the United Nation's emergency assembly addressing this decision. This further proved to be another poorly executed decision by Trump in marginalizing the US from the greater part of the international community.[62] This heedless decision instigated anger and hate towards people of the Jewish faith domestically

---

[60] Collinson & Diamond, September 16, 2016.

[61] Landler, 2017.

[62] Chacar, 2017 & Gaouette, 2017.

and further expanded the divide between Muslims, Jews, Arabs, and Israelis on the global stage.

Muslims

God enjoins justice, and the doing of good, and generosity towards fellow-men; and He forbids all that is shameful and all that runs counter to reason...
-Quran 16:90

Of all the marginalized minorities included in this research, none have faced so much discrimination and attacks as the Muslim community throughout the Trump campaign and into his first year of presidency. In recent years, Muslims have become the most targeted people in the United States with reports of hate crimes continuously increasing towards this group. Due to the events that took place September 11, 2001 and the media's continuous racial profiling of Muslims, xenophobes throughout the country have redirected their hate towards Muslims. Muslim Americans also became the group most targeted by Trump's hate speech and divisive political rhetoric. However, Muslims are an integral part of American society and have been on the land since as far back as American foundational history can be traced. Islam is deeply rooted in American history.

As a matter of fact, Thomas Jefferson's copy of the Quran that was referenced prior to his drafting of the Declaration of Independence was used for swearing in Senator Keith Ellison, the first Muslim to be elected to Congress, and also the first African American elected from Minnesota to serve in the United States House.[63]

Reports of Islam in America dates back to pre-Columbus days indicating that Muslim explorers, mostly Berber-Africans and Moors, had already explored this part of the globe centuries prior to Columbus's infamous voyage to the Americas. Muslims can also be traced back to the Portuguese and Moor explorers that accompanied Columbus on his expedition across the Atlantic.[64] With the spread of Islam throughout North Africa and the Iberian Peninsula, the region consisted of many Muslims, some who took part in Columbus's journey. With the Spanish Inquisition beginning in 1478, many Muslims and Jews were forced to conceal their religious identities in Spain or migrate. Funded by Queen Isabella just after the fall of Muslim Andalusia, Spain, reports of Columbus's crew being racially and religiously diverse indicate that Muslim and African seamen sailed the Great Atlantic in 1492. Once in the new world, some continued to explore and travel west in search of treasures and gold.[65]

---

[63] Robson, 2006.

[64] Curtis, 2009, 4.

[65] Curtis, 2009, 5.

Within a couple of centuries, the transatlantic slave trade would bring more African Muslims to the Americas, however in bondage. Along with explorers, many Africans that were brought to the new world as slaves were Muslim. Most slaves brought to America through the transatlantic slave trade were shipped from West Africa and the Senegambia.[66] Islam was spreading widely in the region at the time and reports of Arabic-speaking Muslim Africans and their stories are recorded. Although rarely referenced, the stories of historical figures such as (Ayuba) Job Ben Solomon and Abdulrahman Ibrahim Ibn Sori, Muslim African slaves, are well documented in American history and serve as clear indicators of the presence of Muslims in early America.[67]

With the abolition of slavery in British colonies and the termination of the transatlantic slave trade by the 19th century, African Muslim slaves were no longer being forced to America. The ones that had already arrived had struggled to maintain their religious identity and beliefs or forced out of their religious practices, converting to Christianity or losing their Muslim identity without embracing another religious practice. However,

---

[66] Curtin, 1972.

[67] Austin, 1997 & Diouf, 2013.

the population of Muslims in America continued to grow through immigration.

Surges of Muslim immigrants can be traced back to the late 1800s and early 1900s. Immigrants have been coming to America for many reasons. Like all other immigrants, Muslims came in search of better opportunities. Many came for economic reasons, while others came in pursuit of education. Some were fleeing war, religious, or political persecution. Others came as seamen and disembarking, residing and building lives in America.[68] Large numbers arrived to New York and intermarried African and Mexican Americans, weaving their ethnicities into the diverse threads of past generations of Americans. With Muslims migrating from Europe and Asia followed by Arab-Muslim immigration, Muslim immigration to the United States is nothing new.

Today, Muslim Americans comprise of an estimated 1% of the United States population.[69] They work in all fields and contribute to American society in education, technology, engineering, science, medicine, business, and government. As all other aforementioned minorities, Muslim Americans have deep-seated roots in American soil.

Migration push and pull factors also contributed to the growth of the Muslim population in America. With the decline of Muslim powers throughout the Middle East, North Africa,

---

[68] Curtis, 2009, 50.

[69] Pew Research Center, 2015.

Europe, and the Asian subcontinent, many Muslim populated nations began to experience a shift in emigration trends. With wars, religious persecution, and political strife impacting these Muslim populated regions, many immigrants were pushed to leave their home countries.[70]

Some were fleeing violence while others sought out better educational and economic opportunities. Compounded by the pull of America's religious liberties, promising future, and lax immigration policies at the time, many Muslims migrated to the US. Many of these early Muslim American immigrants were met with the harsh realities of surviving as first-generation immigrants once they arrived to the country. Moving to a foreign land where the culture, language, beliefs, and way of life was drastically different limited their job opportunities and they struggled for economic survival. Although most of these early immigrants intended on returning to their ethnic lands prior to their emigration, the realities of economic hardship consumed that dream. Instead, they were forced to leave behind parts of their ethnic and religious identities and assimilate into the new world they were a part of.[71] In attempts of blending into mainstream American culture, most changed their names,

---

[70] Smith, 2010, Chapter 3.

[71] Smith, 2010, Chapter 3.

adopting more Euro-Christian sounding conversions instead, and abandoned religious practices they once held dear. Interfaith families slowly stripped younger generations of traditional religious practices and Muslim American immigrants slowly evolved a new cultural identity, that was more American than anything else. [72]

In more recent waves of Muslim immigration, we see large numbers of refugees fleeing war and violence from corrupt and failed states. Although they too suffer similar challenges as early Muslim American immigrants, they have the religious and cultural support of fellow Muslim Americans that have been in America for generations before. In the era of Trump, Muslim Americans have come to learn that the push and pull factors that lead them to their new home country are the points of contention Trump uses to target them in his speech and push forth his Anti-Muslim policies and bans.

Initially, Trump began by calling for a ban against all Muslims entering the United States during his presidential campaign. In March 2016, Trump declared in a CNN interview "Islam hates us," and thereafter issued a call for the surveillance of mosques in the US, and indicated he favored creating a database of Muslims in the US.[73] This language ignited an

---

[72] Smith, 2010, Chapter 3.

[73] Lee, May 23, 2017.

irrational fear towards Muslims that empowered Trump to make promises of policies that would discriminate against this faith group. He went on to attack the family of a Gold Star Army Captain by claiming that the bereaved mother's Muslim faith prevented her from speaking about her son while on stage alongside her grieving husband.

Trump's initial Muslim Ban on the entry of immigrants was signed to ban refugees and immigrants from seven Muslim majority countries. Trump's pompous display of signing the initial executive order quickly spread across national and international news channels as well as social media channels.[74] Although the executive order was clearly unconstitutional and quickly overruled by courts, it sent a message across the globe. It clearly stated that the new American president of the United States held strong anti-Muslim sentiments and would violate sanctified U.S. constitutional rights to fulfill his white supremacist ideologies.

The Muslim Ban in its original form as well as its revised versions, implies that Islam is un-American, and those with Muslim or Arab countries of origin are by default, un-American. Although the first versions of the Muslim ban were rejected by courts, the Trump administration continued pushing forth revised versions that still targeted Muslim majority countries. This caused extensive scrutiny of those traveling from any of the listed countries, including Americans with any

---

[74] Smith, 2017.

connections to countries named on the list. The ban quickly incited an uproar domestically, instigating new reason to question fellow Americans of Middle Eastern descent or Muslim faith and disrupted the lives of legal immigrants that were traveling internationally. Protests at airports broke out across the United States and immigration and civil rights lawyers were spending their time at airports advocating for legal immigrants to be allowed back in to the country.

Once in office, Trump attempted to actualize his ban on Muslims entering the US by signing three executive orders, two of which have been stricken down by Appeals Courts across the nation. His rhetoric, adopted and espoused by his administration, began citing fictitious events as rationale for the ban; events such as the "Bowling Green Massacre," which according to US Counselor to the president, Kellyanne Conway, purported that Muslims attacked and killed Americans, but was never reported on in the media (because no such event had ever occurred); a claim which she was later forced to walk back.

Shortly thereafter, the administration released a list of attempted and successful attacks in the US, which were deemed terrorist attacks, with the list including only non-White perpetrated, mostly Muslim, offenses, a departure from the Obama administration's policy of labeling crimes as terrorism without regard to the race of the perpetrator. Then on May 26, 2017, President Trump issued a statement intended on wishing Muslims a Happy Ramadan, but that included a chastisement and berating of Muslims not doing enough to fight terrorism in three of the four paragraphs of the message.

Orders such as the Muslim Ban do not only impact those living in the US. When the president attempts to carry out executive orders such as this one, he overlooks the fact that Islam is the world's second largest faith and that this narrow-minded approach to our foreign policy speaks volumes to a greater part of the world.[75] It also hinders US relations with our Muslim-majority ally nations such as the United Arab Emirates and Saudi Arabia. When the leader of the world's most powerful country attempts to carry out orders that deem an entire faith group of over 1.6 billion[76] people as un-American, the larger part of the world will naturally deem America as inhuman. This will not only impact our global image, but it will also give rise to anti-American extremist ideologies abroad.

In November 2015, the South Asian Americans Leading Together (SAALT) organization began collecting data on hate crimes targeting minority groups most often associated with Muslim identity. SAALT conducted a study on the impacts of xenophobic political rhetoric towards South Asian, Muslim, Sikh, Hindu, Middle Eastern and Arab communities finding that anti-Muslim violence significantly increased within the time span of Trump's campaign.[77] A collection of xenophobic

---

[75] Desilver & Masci, 2017.

[76] Pew Research Center, 2015.

political rhetoric gathered indicated that 30% of anti-Muslim hate speech came from or was inspired by President-elect Trump.[78] This violent language inspired a surge of aggression targeting those that racially or culturally identify with any characteristics of Muslim identity.

A similar spike of Islamophobic hate is seen to have previously surfaced following the events of September 11, 2001.

> It is not surprising that during the same time period (in the years 2000 through 2006) the American Civil Liberties Union (ACLU) reported that hate crimes against Muslims within the United States rose 674 percent.[79]

As news waves of hate towards Muslims are triggered, those who appear to be Muslim often become the targets of violence. Media reports throughout the country tracked some of these incidents, with many more gone unreported.

---

[77] SAALT, 2017, 3.

[78] SAALT, 2017, 16.

[79] Al Wazni, 2015, 326.

Police and news media reports in recent months have indicated a continued flow of attacks, often against victims wearing traditional Muslim garb or seen as Middle Eastern.[80]

This reality triggered anxieties amongst Muslim communities throughout the country, particularly women in hijab (Muslim headscarf), as they became easy targets for aggression, hate crimes, and acts of discrimination due to the hijab's evident indication of their religious identity. Since the hijab is believed to be a religious mandate for women who adhere to it, hijab-observing women are usually hit the hardest with the brunt of Islamophobic aggression.

Muslim Americans soon found themselves in a sociopolitical environment in which the average Muslim, and veiled Muslim women in particular, had to defend themselves against the perception of Islam as being both oppressive and violent. This perception of Muslim women persists; CAIR recently published a study that not only found Islamophobia to be on the rise, but also found that hate crimes and acts of violence are

---

[80] Lichtblau, September 17, 2016.

more often directed at Muslim women, who wear the hijab, than Muslim men.[81]

Extreme acts of Islamophobic violence have further contributed to the growing number of crimes including murder, arson, physical assault, and other forms of harassment, particularly when they are dismissed as general crimes and not identified as hate crimes. In February 2015, Deah Barakat (23), and his wife Yusor Abu-Salha (21), along with her sister Razan Abu-Salha (19) were shot and killed, by their neighbor 45 year old Craig Hicks in their condominium home in Chapel Hill, North Carolina. The three young college students expressed fears for their safety to relatives due to Hicks's harassment of them prior to their murders. Yusor, who wore hijab, moved in to the complex with her newly-wed husband Deah. She was confronted by Hicks prior to her murder, being told that he did not like the way she looked. Although many neighbors in the complex stated that Hicks embodied an intimidating attitude within the neighborhood, he felt emboldened to commit a heinous act of violence against the couple and Yusor's visiting younger sister due to the Abu-Salha's visibly evident Muslim attire. Hicks had expressed his hate for religious expression through his Facebook social media account and followed up by fatally shooting the three young students, execution style, in their home. Although initial reports presented this case as a

---

[81] Al Wazni, 2015, 326.

mere parking dispute, it is evident through further investigation
that the hijabs the sisters wore incited Hicks to take his
aggression to an extreme level.

> But the head scarves that Abu-Salha and her
> sister wore signaled their religion. Judging by
> Hicks's Facebook page, any display of faith
> infuriated him.[82]

This was a clear indicator of Hicks's Islamophobic motives to
commit a heinous crime against his young neighbors.
Furthermore, Kennedy law Professor at Chapel Hill states

> It can be easier to commit violence against
> someone who is an other. Prejudice is one of the
> easiest ways to dehumanize someone.[83]

Islamophobia is based on the notion that Muslims are not a
thread of the fabric of American society, and thus Muslims are
excluded from the mainstream, in this case, deemed unworthy of
life due to the apparent visibility of their faith.
Jack McDevitt, a criminologist at Northeastern
University who studies hate crimes, reveals why the Chapel Hill
Shooting should be identified as one.

---

[82] Talbot, June 22, 2015.

[83] Talbot, June 22, 2015.

> In this case, he's angry about the way people
> around him live, but he's chosen these specific
> people because they also represent a religion he's
> intolerant of.[84]

According to McDevitt, one factor that the F.B.I. considers when assessing a possible hate crime is whether "the level of violence is more than what is required to do the crime."[85] On that note, the fact that Hicks fired a number of shots and pressed his gun to the women's heads seems relevant.

Other reports of Islamophobic hate crimes have been emerging across the nation, with vandalism of mosques, mosque arson, and cases of violent physical assault and harassment accompanied by Islamophobic rhetoric. The 2016 Presidential race has left its legacy of Islamophobic rhetoric, fueled by negative perceptions of the religion through mainstream media, aiding candidate Donald Trump in winning the election. Trump's outspoken bigotry and rhetoric of Muslims normalized hate towards the minority group. His inciting of violence against those who oppose his views during the campaign further emboldened Islamophobes and racists across the nation to carry out acts of aggression and violence towards vulnerable minorities. Immediately following his November election,

---

[84] Talbot, June 22, 2015.

[85] Talbot, June 22, 2015.

reports of harassment and violence particularly towards women in hijab were reported throughout different states.

> We're seeing these stereotypes and derogative statements become part of the political discourse," said Brian Levin, the director of the Center for the Study of Hate and Extremism at the San Bernardino campus. "The bottom line is we're talking about a significant increase in these types of hate crimes." He said that the frequency of anti-Muslim violence appeared to have increased immediately after some of Mr. Trump's most incendiary comments.[86]

Furthermore, the ACLU has received hundreds of reports of incidents where Muslim women have been denied their rights, harassed, denied employment due to their religious identity and appearance, prevented from extracurricular activities and athletic events, forced to remove their religious attire in jails and courthouses, denied access to certain public facilities, such as pools, malls, and public buildings.[87]

Along with the incitement of direct violence, political opponents vied for votes with promises for the implementation of structurally violent policies targeting Muslims or minorities

---

[86] Lichtblau, September 17, 2016.

[87] ACLU, 2008.

often perceived as Muslim. With political leaders normalizing hate speech and transforming it into official systematic policy, hate groups felt empowered and hate crimes towards Muslims and related minorities soared. The direct result of this rhetoric was that hate crimes against Muslims increased by 67% (according to the Federal Bureau of Investigation) from 2014 to 2015, the year Trump commenced his campaign.[88]

History reveals that people of all faiths and colors have always played a major role in great global shifts, yet white supremacists and ethnocentrics continue to omit the details that show the relevance of other races or faiths in the making of American history. Today, most Americans have internalized these racially and religiously exclusive narratives and are ignorant of these historical foundational realities.

---

[88] US Department of Justice, 2015.

Ideologies Drive Policies

We may have different religions, different languages, different colored skin,
but we all belong to one human race.
-Kofi Annan

The Problem with White Supremacy

No culture can live if it attempts to be exclusive.
-Mahatma Gandhi

White Supremacy is an ideology based around the notion that the white race is superior to all other races, particularly in relation to those who identify as black. Skin color is used as a measuring standard towards the treatment of people; the lighter skinned a person or group is, the closer they resemble those of white European descent and therefore the less inferior they are deemed by white supremacists and the less chance of them falling victim to aggression caused by this ideology. It is a bigoted belief that is the root to many of the racist and discriminatory behaviors and policies enacted towards people of color. Not only does it impact policy, causing structural violence, it also manifests itself through acts of direct violence to people who don't pass as white. People who are visibly different than the image set by white supremacists either by shade of skin or religious attire, such as the Jewish yamaka or a Muslim hijab, are usually targets of white supremacist violence. White supremacist terrorism accounts for 73% of violent extremist attacks resulting in death following September 11,

2001.[89] However, the highly skewed misrepresentation of
terrorism in the media suggests that Islamist terrorists are the
most severe threat faced by the US. A study conducted by the
University of Alabama reveals that attacks by Muslims receive
357% more media coverage than attacks by non-Muslims,
including white supremacists.[90] While in reality, a 2005 FBI
report reveals that 94% of terror attacks in the US between 1980
to 2005 (including the events of September 11, 2001) were
carried out by non-Muslims.[91] This FBI report also indicates that
more acts of terrorism were carried out by Latinos (42%),
Extreme Left Wing Groups (24%), and Jews (7%) than Muslims
(6%).[92] With the media's gross misrepresentation of this reality
perpetuating stereotypes of Muslim extremists being the greatest
threat of terrorism in the US, cultural violence ensues,
misdirecting the focus of where the most significant threat of
terrorism in the US actually lies. According to the warnings

---

[89] Government Accountability Office, 2017.

[90] Kearns, Betus, & Lemieux, 2017.

[91] US Department of Justice, 2005.

[92] US Department of Justice, 2005.

issued by the FBI and Department of Homeland Security, that threat is actually white supremacist groups.[93]

Places of worship and neighborhoods with high concentration of minorities are also commonly targeted by individuals associated with these white extremist groups through hate crimes involving acts of vandalism, arson, physical violence or systematic policies that aim to keep the communities marginalized. Conversely, when people who hold white supremacist ideologies are elected into office, their violence towards minority groups is manifested in different forms and carried out from a higher level. It is emboldened, given a platform to exercise, and has an indirect, yet greater detriment on society. These bigoted officials are then able to act upon these xenophobic beliefs through systems of institutionalized racism, structural violence, and marginalization policies.

The constant struggle of coping with such various forms of racism and discrimination often takes a significant psychological and emotional toll on many of these targeted people. In 2003, researcher William Smith of the University of Utah coined the term *racial battle fatigue*[94] upon his findings from a study on the impacts of racially charged micro-aggressions towards black male students in predominantly white

---

[93] Winter, 2017.

[94] Racial Battle Fatigue: the emotional, physical, and psychological toll a person of color experiences due to constant discrimination, micro-aggressions, and stereotype threat.

universities.[95] Through surveys and interviews, Smith gathered data from 36 students throughout the United States regarding the racial stressors they face and the toll these stressors take on them. The study revealed that black males and people of color face daily micro-aggressions that build up and have a taxing impact on their productivity, overall well-being, and potential for success. This is excluding policies, quotas, and structural forms of marginalization that minority communities face. Through this study, we see how the cultural acceptance of white supremacist ideologies weave into the fabric of a society and succeed in marginalizing minorities that identify as anything but white. Although the ideology may not be specifically incorporated into the law, it finds its way into the marginalization of groups through psychological conditioning and micro-aggressive social behaviors.

White privilege (also known as *white skin privilege*) refers to the societal privileges that people with light skin benefit from simply for the color of their skin. This form of social discrimination is manifested as preferential treatment and bias in favor of those who pass as white. It includes the ease of access to opportunities that allow for upward social mobility, career and educational advancement as a default standard for whites, general presumptions of innocence for light skinned individuals, and social validation of all forms. Oftentimes, it is so deeply engrained in the psyche of individuals because of a lifetime of conditioning and living stereotypes about non-whites

---

[95] Smith, 2007.

in the pre-dominant culture, that people don't realize how much they benefit from the light shade of their skin. Due to the deep roots of white supremacy most people are blinded of its reality, believing that racism only exists when direct acts of aggression are inflicted on minorities. This is misleading as it dismisses the hierarchies of power that play into amplifying white voices and silencing those of other groups. In 1988, Researcher Peggy McIntosh published an article about male privilege and how her research led to her findings on white privilege. She compiled a list of daily privileges enjoyed by those who identify as white that hold people of color back in different aspects of social, economic, and educational growth.[96] Her research further informed how race silently fuels inequitable privilege, limits access to opportunity for some, and hinders equal attainability of success.

Colorism, discrimination based on the color or shade of a person's skin, is a widespread reality plaguing all parts of the world. From the Indian subcontinent, to different parts of Africa, to the Middle East, countries throughout the globe suffer from colorism. Popular advertisements for beauty care products such as "Fair & Lovely", a skin bleaching cream, to hair care products that lighten or drastically straighten naturally curly, thick, or afro hair, are small indicators of a society's favorability for a certain physical appearance; in this case lighter skin and

---

[96] McIntosh, 1988.

straighter hair-physical traits usually attributed to whiteness.[97] The discussions surrounding the negative impacts of some of these beauty care products on human health reveal the costs people are willing to endure to achieve these perceived standards of beauty in their pursuit of social acceptability.[98] Movements to appreciate the beauty of natural afro-textured hair or darker shades of skin have spread to eradicate the effects of colorism on the standards of beauty particularly in the US. In many cultures, it is common to hear conversations about beauty in reference to having lighter skin or limper hair.

These deeply engrained notions of beauty and acceptable physical appearance throughout the world stem from a long history of white supremacy. These sentiments suggest that whiter is better and lighter is whiter; consequently, constructing the perception that lighter is inherently better. These long inherited social biases that grant some privileges and create others challenges can all be rooted back to the fallacy that there exists a hierarchy of races within the human race, and that whiteness is at the top.

Attire that is commonly associated with that of white people is also often perceived as being more socially acceptable and attributed to success and privilege. Any indicator of whiteness earns a non-white individual privileges that would otherwise be withheld had they not expressed their proximity to whiteness. This too, is rooted in white supremacist ideologies.

---

[97] Banerji, January 28, 2016 & Senanayake, July 31, 2018.

[98] Banerji, January 28, 2016 & Senanayake, July 31, 2018.

Colorism is so deeply ingrained in US perceptions of appearance. It is common for men and women in public as well as professional spaces to be scrutinized based on their attire, physical appearance, or noncompliance of white standards of acceptable appearance. Reports of African-American women being told to change their natural afro-hair to appear more professional[99] or Muslim women in hijab being denied jobs or being asked to remove their Islamic head covering at the work place are just a few of the many incidents in which we see the ripple effects of colorism and white supremacy on a cultural level in America.

We also see a similar phenomenon occur with cultural and linguistic identifiers of being white. Languages other than those associated with white European heritage face more scrutiny. Speakers having an accent that indicates they primarily speak a foreign language or using those languages publicly face excessive forms of linguistic discrimination and profiling. Although linguistic discrimination is outlawed in the US under the umbrella of Titles VI and VII of the Civil Rights Act of 1964 which prohibits discrimination on the basis of race, color, or national origin, many people with foreign accents or varying languages regularly report mistreatment in public spaces due to their diverse language use. This prejudice is also experienced by English speakers who speak with an accent that socially distances them from the white majority. For instance, those who speak African American Vernacular English, English with

---

[99] Webb, July 20, 2015.

Hispanic, Arabic, or Asian accents, will often face more discrimination than those whose English is more commonly associated with that perceived to be spoken by white individuals. Studies have been conducted to observe the real consequences of language prejudice on marginalized people and findings indicated that those perceived to sound "white" were given preferential treatment.[100] One study conducted on the leasing of property by landlords revealed that prospective tenants were turned away simply because they did not sound "white" over the phone when calling about property rentals.[101] Cases of passengers on airplanes being removed from their flights for speaking Arabic have also been reported.[102] Other forms of linguistic profiling and discrimination occur in workplaces, legal testimonies, educational institutions, and other public spaces.

A person of color who speaks a dialect of English more closely related to that which is commonly spoken by white Americans is perceived as "being white", or coming to closer proximity of whiteness. This too often attracts certain privileges to individuals who are able to master that way of speaking and is often employed as a means of moving up the social mobility ladder among minorities. Although often overlooked as a form

---

[100] Baugh, 2003.

[101] Baugh, 2003.

[102] Stack, 2016 & CAIR Webmaster 2018.

of prejudice, linguistic discrimination is a symptom of the perceived hierarchies of ethnicity and race.

The ideology of white supremacy contradicts the American constitution and undermines the pillars of justice and equality the nation was established upon. With the United States being a land of liberty and peace for all, there is no space for ideologies that favor one race or ethnic heritage above all others. We cannot sustain a nation built upon the foundations of religious freedom and diversity with beliefs that deem entire faith groups or races as targets for hostility. White supremacy is un-American and causes a divisive rift throughout a nation built on the shoulders of diversity.

Embracing the differences that weave the tapestry of this nation will no doubt build a stronger, more resilient foundation for the prosperity of this country. Through a healthy appreciation of diversity, learning from the differences amongst Americans can cultivate a deeper understanding of the differences across the globe, enhancing our international relations and transforming the way America is viewed by the rest of the world. White supremacy and indications of it obstruct America's potential from achieving the highest level of liberty and equality, and essentially, limits its ability to reach the heights of greatness.

Research

People create social conditions and people can change them.
-Tess Onwueme

Problem

Trump's campaign and ongoing hate speech is marginalizing minorities in the United States and creating a negative view of the United States of America to the rest of the world. Minorities in any country face an uphill battle in asserting their rights and constantly struggle for acceptance by the societies in which they live. They face intolerance continuously as the vicious cycles of discrimination and violence come and go. Minorities are often scapegoated unjustly when anything in a nation goes wrong. Any drastic change in a country's economy, national policies, or demographics poses a perceived cultural threat to the majority population. This triggers a re-emergence of previously buried sentiments of racism, xenophobia, misogyny, Islamophobia, and anti-Semitism, feelings of racial, ethnic, or gender superiority that were believed to have been resolved in past cycles of social intolerance resurface in the views of society, causing a new series of violence and discrimination targeting the most vulnerable minority groups. Politicians have exploited the fears of the majority populations to fuel their campaigns and win votes. President Donald Trump particularly capitalized on this distasteful campaigning strategy to win the 2016 presidential election. Whereas in the past, waves of discrimination were usually instigated by major acts of injustice or drastic events, the main reason for the 2015-2017 spikes of violence and negative public sentiments targeting minority groups has been directly attributed to the 2016 presidential Campaign.[103]

Following the 2016 presidential campaign of repeatedly negative rhetoric against minorities, the FBI released its annual Hate Crimes Report and revealed that hate crimes had surged by a whopping 7%; from 5462 in 2014 to 5850 in 2015.[104] The following year, reports continued to rise to 6121 incidents reported in 2016.[105] To directly link the rise of hate crimes to the political rhetoric, we need to examine the surrounding political events that may have spurred the violence to erupt. The rise in violence towards specific groups or changes in policies that target particular minorities will inform the impact of Trump's hostile language towards these people.

---

[103] Bouie, 2016.

[104] US Department of Justice, 2015.

[105] US Department of Justice, 2017.

Methods

An analysis of hate crime reports gathered over the past four presidential terms will reveal the impact of each political leader's presence on society's sentiments towards particular groups. The fluctuation of hate crimes towards certain groups will inform us on the change of public hostility towards these groups over the years. Assessing the change in levels of hostility towards minorities throughout the terms being studied in relation to major events that occurred will determine the measure of impact these events had on public sentiments towards groups. Of these events, the catastrophic attacks of September 11th, 2001 are included.

The data gathered are based on reported incidents of discrimination or violence that targeted the aforementioned groups. Reports of a spike in hate crimes targeting groups Trump rebuked during his campaign or offenders attributing the motivation for their crimes to Trump speeches or his policy changes are considered evidence of indications of Trump's rhetoric inciting violence towards minority groups. Due to a variation in minority populations, hate crime reports were plotted based on their percentage of change to demonstrate how the events that unfolded each year affected the levels of hostility each minority group faced. These findings are displayed in graphs and tables found under the *Findings and Data Analysis* section of this research.

Data gathered through surveys conducted regarding negative opinions and reports of violence towards domestic minority groups that were targeted by Trump's negative rhetoric and post-election discriminatory policy changes also inform the findings of this study. Survey and poll data collected from national think tanks and social service organizations that service targeted minority groups as well as civil rights and anti-discrimination organizations are incorporated into the findings. These data are plotted along line graphs spread out over years, corresponding with elaborations on the sequence of national events that may have spurred variations in the data. An examination of events in which Trump publicly issued statements vilifying minority groups will also be included as national events that may have triggered any changes. Events are selected based on an observation of media reports, survey findings of well-reputed organizations, and critical issues that were most prevalently discussed throughout the years.

A comparative analysis is then done to evaluate the impact of Trump's hate speech on domestic stability, international relations, and security based on the data found as opposed to the results found during past presidential leadership. Based on those findings, conclusions regarding Trump's political language and the impact it has on national stability and international security for the United States are drawn.

Data are gathered from organizations including the Federal Bureau of Investigation (FBI), the Institute for Social Policy and Understanding (ISPU), American Civil Liberty Union (ACLU), South Asian Americans Leading Together (SAALT), and the Pew Research Center.

The FBI releases an annual publication of data on hate crimes that are reported across the country based on an array of traits. Of those, race, ethnicity, gender, and religion are included. A selection of this collection of data was used to compare the variation in reports of hate crimes prior to Trump's campaign, to the year of its commencement, 2015, and into the year of his election, 2016.

The ISPU is a well-established think tank that collects data that impacts Muslim Americans. It was established in 2002 and continues to be one of the most significant databases for gathering information pertaining to the Muslim American community. Considering that much of Trump's immigration and foreign policies, along with his political rhetoric directly and significantly impacted the Muslim American minority, ISPU serves as a reliable and relevant source for gathering data for this study.

The ACLU was founded in 1920 to preserve civil rights of all Americans and offer protection from the abuse of power and violation of constitutional rights by the government against citizens. It has become a well-reputed organization at the forefront of the fight to preserve civil liberties. This organization has a history of civil rights advocacy and a history of reports tracking violations of civil rights by the government. The ACLU has been addressing Trump's efforts at implementing unconstitutional policies targeting all minority groups and has compiled data on all related incidents since the beginning of the Trump campaign.

SAALT is a non-profit organization that works towards racial justice and civil rights advocacy for South Asians. Due to Trump's emphasis on anti-Muslim rhetoric and the large number of Muslim South-Asian Americans as well as the overwhelming resemblance of South-Asian Americans with Muslim and Arab Americans, SAALT has conducted a research to gather statistics regarding the growth of hate towards this minority group during the 2016 Presidential campaign.

The Pew Research Center provides empirical evidence on opinions as well as reports of violence that minorities experienced throughout the era of Trump's campaign and his first year in office. Pew Research Center is well-reputed for its non-biased, fact-based, and highly credible statistical reporting that is often referenced regarding policy making domestically as well as internationally. Data gathered from the Pew Research Center's database is generally recognized as highly reliable and valued.

Reports from major news sources such as *CNN* and *The New York Times* have also been referenced for the sake of this study. Since media plays an integral part in influencing public opinion, observing news sources are key to this study. The data gathered are analyzed and used to draw conclusions about the impact of Trump's political rhetoric on the aforementioned minorities. Statistics of hate crimes reported over the past four presidential terms serve as the primary measuring tool in this study for the effects of negative rhetoric on minority groups. An investigation of the data in relation to national events will inform whether specific domestic issues were addressed by past presidents in a manner that may have triggered the insurgence of violence towards minorities that reported a change in number of hate crimes. For instance, due to the significant increase in crimes targeting Muslims in 2001, I investigated the language used by President Bush during that time in addressing the terrorist attacks of September 11, 2001. I researched news articles to assess President Bush's approach in regard to the national crisis and compared it to the language use of Trump regarding issues of terrorism. The statistics reported for the 2015 and 2016 hate crimes towards Muslims following Trump's rhetoric inform the impact of presidential language on the public.

Similar findings for other mentioned minority groups such as African-Americans, Hispanic-Americans, and Jews are also included. The findings reveal the impacts, if any, of President Trump's hostile rhetoric towards these groups. This information is then projected to shed light on the international perception of America's image and any lasting effects Trump's language will have on international relations. It is also used to assess the role Trump's rhetoric played in pushing discriminatory policy changes towards the mentioned groups and how these policy changes impacted Americans domestically as well as America abroad.

After analyzing the data, if there is little to no significant statistical evidence of violence or weakening of America's international perception resulting from Trump's rhetoric, then it can be concluded that Trump's political rhetoric and hate speech does not impact national stability or international relations. This

would indicate that Trump's rhetoric is not as harmful as
originally hypothesized to be. On the other hand, if a
correlation between national violence, international security, and
Trump's choice of language is found, then it can be concluded
that hate speech by political leaders can incite acts of domestic
violence and threaten international stability.

Limitations

      This research will be limited to existing statistics on reported crimes against minorities over the last decade and a half. Data on hate crimes are often inaccurate due to a variety of reasons. Many victims of such crimes often do not come forward and report these crimes due to fear or lack of support. Many of the crimes that are reported are dismissed as minor offenses and not categorized as hate crimes motivated by prejudice when they often are due to a lack of evidence regarding the motivation or an aim at a lesser sentencing for the offender. Due to this reality, many of the statistics reporting on crimes committed towards minority groups are often under-representative of their reality. Furthermore, since undocumented immigrants are a large number of those targeted by Trump's speech and many consequent hate crimes; the fear of deportation prevents them from reporting incidents of violence they experience. Minorities in general tend to experience higher levels of fear and distrust towards law enforcement and are more reluctant to report crimes. This undoubtedly hinders the ability to gather an accurate measure of data regarding the impact of Trump's rhetoric on minority groups in the United States. Another limitation regarding the data used for this study include the amount of data available at the time of the study. Considering that this research has been conducted within the first year of Trump's presidential term, hate crimes statistics for the year 2017 were unavailable as of the date of this research and the impacts of his first year of leadership could not be thoroughly measured. The data are limited to the hate crime reports available throughout his campaign and election year and we must rely on other means of assessing impact for the years that follow.

Another limitation of this study is regarding the classification of those targeted by hate crimes. Minorities with Middle Eastern and North African roots are categorized as "white" on most national databases, and in the FBI's record of hate crime reports. This drastically impacts the findings because these groups do not visibly identify as white and are often targeted due to their non-white physical identity through hate crimes. However, their attacks are often reported under the classification of anti-white incidents due to a classification of their ethnic roots being categorizes as white. This detracts from the data that could inform anti-Muslim sentiments and inaccurately feeds into higher reports of hate-crimes fueled by anti-white sentiments

It is important to effectively and critically analyze the data gathered for this research in relation to other reports available and events unfolding to ensure that it is interpreted in a way that best reveals the impact of Trump's rhetoric on marginalized minorities and domestic stability rather than its influence merely on public opinion. This can be done effectively by concentrating our conclusions on the statistics of the crimes, analysis of polls, and the effects of policy changes that have followed his campaign and presidency.

Findings and Data Analysis

The data reveal the impact of Trump's language on minorities and America's global image. The series of events that took place starting in 2015 during Trump's campaign influenced events that unfolded on into the year after. The data evidently reveal that Trump's hate-inspired comments directly incited people towards violence. The statistics bare the change in violence towards minorities as Trump began his campaign. We start with data at the beginning of President George W. Bush's term in 2000. The data demonstrate that hate crimes reached an all-time high in the year 2001. It is evident that the events of September 11, 2001 played a significant role in these results. As we assess the data thoroughly, it is important to keep in mind that different minorities throughout the country comprise of different sizes of the population.

Table 1 gives a breakdown of population sizes of the US demography based on recent collections of data through the US Census and Pew Research Center. It is important to note that the white category includes many people who don't physically identify as mainstream white. For instance, Arabs, Lebanese, and Moroccans are often targeted in anti-Muslim violence, however, they may identify as white based on US Census data. Therefore, categorizing hate crimes may not be as accurate as we would like. Furthermore, because different size populations constitute different minorities, the impact of violence specifically targeting each group may have a larger magnitude depending on the size of the minority population. For instance, looking at Table 3 may give the impression that Whites were more severely impacted by hate in 2001 than Muslims were because the number of anti-White incidents was nearly twice as much as anti-Muslim, however, because Muslims are a very small minority of the US, only about 1%, the magnitude of the hate targeting this minority is much greater. Violence directed at this minority is impacting a greater proportion of its population than that of a much larger group. Therefore, using percentages of change also serves as a useful measure of assessing hate trends over the years.

Incidents reported on the following tables and figures are based on data collected from the FBI's National Annual Hate Crime Reports.

<table>
<tr><td colspan="3" align="center">Table 1</td></tr>
<tr><td colspan="3" align="center">US Demographic Populations[106] by Minority</td></tr>
<tr><td align="center">Minority Group</td><td align="center">Most Recent Minority Population Estimates</td><td align="center">Percentages</td></tr>
<tr><td align="center">White[107]</td><td align="center">248,485,057[108]</td><td align="center">76.90%</td></tr>
<tr><td align="center">Black</td><td align="center">45,672,250[109]</td><td align="center">14.13%</td></tr>
<tr><td align="center">Hispanic</td><td align="center">58,000,000[110]</td><td align="center">17.95%</td></tr>
<tr><td align="center">Jews</td><td align="center">5,700,000[111]</td><td align="center">1.76%</td></tr>
<tr><td align="center">Muslims</td><td align="center">3,300,000</td><td align="center">1.02%</td></tr>
<tr><td align="center">Females</td><td align="center">164,148,777</td><td align="center">50.80%[112]</td></tr>
<tr><td align="center">Total US Population</td><td align="center">323,127,513[113]</td><td align="center">100%[114]</td></tr>
</table>

---

[106] Calculations are estimates based on data available.

[107] "White: A person having origins in any of the original peoples of Europe, the Middle East, or North Africa. It includes people who indicate their race as "White" or report entries such as Irish, German, Italian, Lebanese, Arab, Moroccan, or Caucasian." (US Census, 2014).

[108] US Census, 2014.

[109] US Census, 2014.

[110] Pew Research Center, 2017.

[111] Pew Research Center, 2013.

[112] US Census, 2016.

[113] US Census, 2014.

[114] Totals may not add up to exactly one hundred percent.

Table 2 and Figure 1 display the trends of hate crimes reported across the country from the year 2000 until the year of Trump's election, 2016. A sharp rise in hate crimes peaks in the year 2001. This is likely due to the events of 9/11 that are believed to have provoked many Americans to direct their frustrations and fears towards Muslims. However, after the decline of reported hate incidents in 2001, we see hate crimes peaking again in 2008, the year President Obama was elected into office, and after steady decline, incidents again begin to rise in 2015 and 2016, the years Trump leaderships began to surface.

Table 2	
Total Annual Hate Crimes	
Year	**Incidents Reported**
2000	8063
2001	9730
2002	7462
2003	7489
2004	7,649
2005	7,163
2006	7,722
2007	7,624
2008	7,783
2009	6,604
2010	6,628
2011	6,222
2012	5,796
2013	5,928
2014	5,479
2015	5,850
2016	6,121

Figure 1

Table 3 and Figure 2 display the number of incidents targeting the different groups throughout the country from 2000-2016. It is evident that Black or African Americans suffer the most hate incidents across the country, however, hate targeting this group is at a steady decline. In 2008, we see the incidents targeting Black/African Americans increased drastically after steadily declining in relation to the first black president being elected into office. Following Obama's inauguration, hate crimes dropped and continued to drop at a significant rate, particularly towards Black/African Americans. This reveals a lot about the effect of political leadership and its impact on

Table 3					
Hate Crime Reports by Group Bias					
Bias Motivation **Year**	**Anti-White ***	**Anti-Black**	**Anti-Hispanic**	**Anti-Jewish**	**Anti-Muslim**	**Anti-Female**
2000	875	2884	557	1109	28	N/A
2001	891	2899	597	1043	481	N/A
2002	719	2486	480	931	155	N/A
2003	830	2548	426	927	149	N/A
2004	829	2731	475	954	156	N/A
2005	828	2630	522	848	128	N/A
2006	890	2640	576	967	156	N/A
2007	749	2658	595	969	115	N/A
2008	716	2876	561	1013	105	N/A
2009	545	2284	483	931	107	N/A
2010	575	2201	534	887	160	N/A
2011	504	2076	405	771	157	N/A
2012	657	1805	384	674	130	N/A
2013	653	1856	331	625	135	N/A
2014	593	1621	299	609	154	23
2015	613	1745	299	664	257	16
2016	760	1739	344	684	307	24

*WHITE includes people having origins in Europe, the Middle East, or North Africa. It includes those of Irish, German, Italian, Lebanese, Arab, Moroccan, or Caucasian descent.

minority groups in the US. It sheds light onto Trump's impact regarding 2015-2016 hate crime trends.

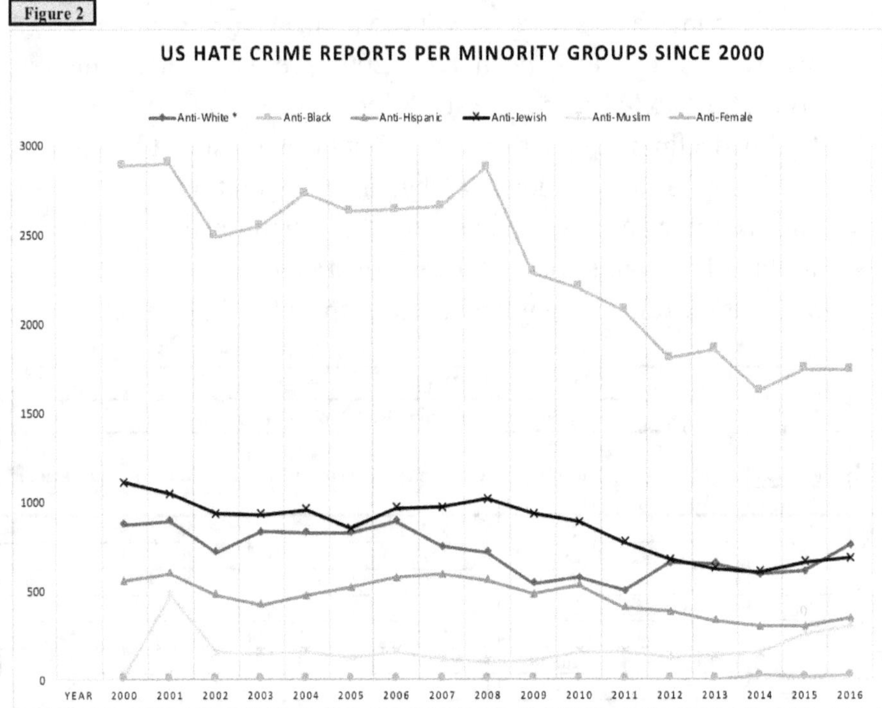

Although Black/African American hate incidents are higher than any other minority, Table 4 shows that Black/African American hate is decreasing at an average rate of about 2.75% a year, dropping from 2884 to 1621 reported incidents a year, until the year Trump launched his divisive campaign. In 2015, anti-Black incidents began to rise again after following a decline.

Table 4 and Figure 3 of our data demonstrate that the highest percent increase of hate crimes from the year 2000 to 2001 were towards Muslims. With an astounding increase of nearly 1618% in hate crime incidents targeting Muslims that year, it is evident that this minority group became the central focus for negative public sentiment following the events of 9/11 and the media's coverage of the War on Terror. Along with hate crimes, many discriminatory policies targeting this minority (including government initiatives of countering violent extremism through the excessive, unwarranted surveillance of Muslim communities) continued to perpetuate hate towards this small group. Table 4 and Figure 3 display the impact on each minority over the 16 years being studied. As all other minority groups declined in hate crime incidents throughout the first four presidential terms of the 21st Century, we see that hate incidents targeting Muslims continued to rise with an average increase of 103.5% over the 16 years.

Table 4										
Percent of Change of Hate Crimes for Each Group										
	Anti-White *		Anti-Black		Anti-Hispanic		Anti-Jewish		Anti-Muslim	
Year	Incidents	Percent change	Incidents	Percent change	Incidents	Percent change	Incidents	Percent change	Incidents	Percent change
2000	875		2884		557		1109		28	
2001	891	1.83%	2899	0.52%	597	7.18%	1043	-5.95%	481	1617.86%
2002	719	-19.30%	2486	-14.25%	480	-19.60%	931	-10.74%	155	-67.78%
2003	830	15.44%	2548	2.49%	426	-11.25%	927	-0.43%	149	-3.87%
2004	829	-0.12%	2731	7.18%	475	11.50%	954	2.91%	156	4.70%
2005	828	-0.12%	2630	-3.70%	522	9.89%	848	-11.11%	128	-17.95%
2006	890	7.49%	2640	0.38%	576	10.34%	967	14.03%	156	21.88%
2007	749	-15.84%	2658	0.68%	595	3.30%	969	0.21%	115	-26.28%
2008	716	-4.41%	2876	8.20%	561	-5.71%	1013	4.54%	105	-8.70%
2009	545	-23.88%	2284	-20.58%	483	-13.90%	931	-8.09%	107	1.90%
2010	575	5.50%	2201	-3.63%	534	10.56%	887	-4.73%	160	49.53%
2011	504	-12.35%	2076	-5.68%	405	-24.16%	771	-13.08%	157	-1.88%
2012	657	30.36%	1805	-13.05%	384	-5.19%	674	-12.58%	130	-17.20%
2013	653	-0.61%	1856	2.83%	331	-13.80%	625	-7.27%	135	3.85%
2014	593	-9.19%	1621	-12.66%	299	-9.67%	609	-2.56%	154	14.07%
2015	613	3.37%	1745	7.65%	299	0.00%	664	9.03%	257	66.88%
2016	760	23.98%	1739	-0.34%	344	15.05%	684	3.01%	307	19.46%
Percent of Change Averages over 16 years	0.13%		-2.75%		-2.22%		-2.68%		103.53%	

*WHITE includes people having origins in Europe, the Middle East, or North Africa. It includes those of Irish, German, Italian, Lebanese, Arab, Moroccan, or Caucasian descent.

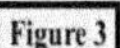

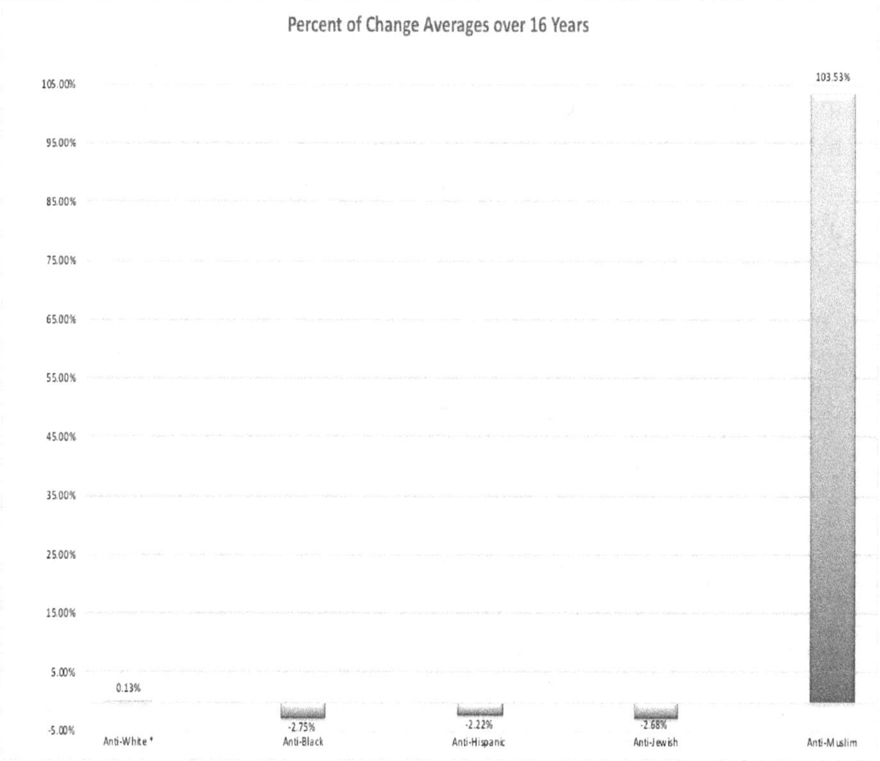

Percent of Change Averages over 16 Years

Table 5 and Figure 4 display the percentages of change in hate crimes over the 16 years analyzed. This shows the trends for each minority painting a clearer image of the impacts of hate on each group. It is apparent that Muslims are the group most impacted by an increase of hate over the 16 years of this study.

Table 5					
Percent of Change of Hate Crimes for Each Group					
Year	**Anti-White***	**Anti-Black**	**Anti-Hispanic**	**Anti-Jewish**	**Anti-Muslim**
2000					
2001	1.83%	0.52%	7.18%	-5.95%	1617.86%
2002	-19.30%	-14.25%	-19.60%	-10.74%	-67.78%
2003	15.44%	2.49%	-11.25%	-0.43%	-3.87%
2004	-0.12%	7.18%	11.50%	2.91%	4.70%
2005	-0.12%	-3.70%	9.89%	-11.11%	-17.95%
2006	7.49%	0.38%	10.34%	14.03%	21.88%
2007	-15.84%	0.68%	3.30%	0.21%	-26.28%
2008	-4.41%	8.20%	-5.71%	4.54%	-8.70%
2009	-23.88%	-20.58%	-13.90%	-8.09%	1.90%
2010	5.50%	-3.63%	10.56%	-4.73%	49.53%
2011	-12.35%	-5.68%	-24.16%	-13.08%	-1.88%
2012	30.36%	-13.05%	-5.19%	-12.58%	-17.20%
2013	-0.61%	2.83%	-13.80%	-7.27%	3.85%
2014	-9.19%	-12.66%	-9.67%	-2.56%	14.07%
2015	3.37%	7.65%	0.00%	9.03%	66.88%
2016	23.98%	-0.34%	15.05%	3.01%	19.46%
*WHITE includes people having origins in Europe, the Middle East, or North Africa. It includes those of Irish, German, Italian, Lebanese, Arab, Moroccan, or Caucasian descent.					

Figure 4

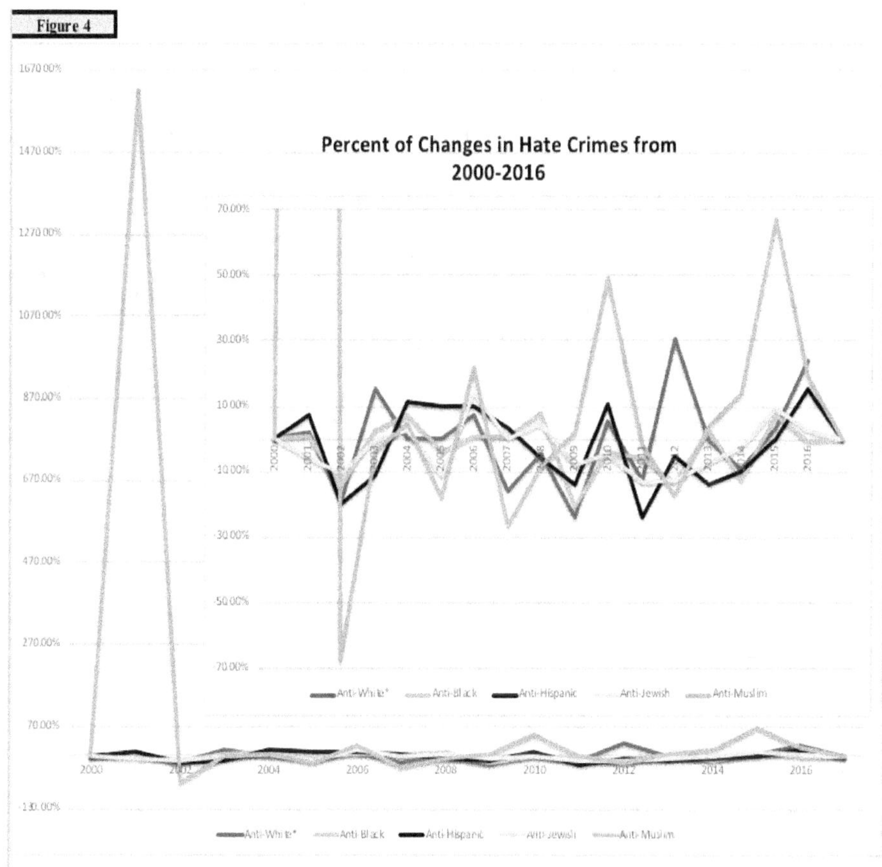

Percent of Changes in Hate Crimes from 2000-2016
1670.00%
1470.00%
1270.00%
1070.00%
870.00%
670.00%
470.00%
270.00%
70.00%
-130.00%
70.00%
50.00%
30.00%
10.00%
-10.00%
-30.00%
-50.00%
-70.00%
Anti-White* Anti-Black Anti-Hispanic Anti-Jewish Anti-Muslim
2000 2004 2006 2008 2010 2012 2014 2016
Anti-White* Anti-Black Anti-Hispanic Anti-Jewish Anti-Muslim

Tables 6-10 and Figures 5-9 give a closer look of these trends throughout each presidential term. Again, we can see that the greatest spike of hate, despite the fluctuation, is experienced by Muslims and continues to increase with Trump's election.

Table 6				
Hate Crime Trends During First Bush Administration				
Year	Anti-White	Anti-Black	Anti-Hispanic	Anti-Jewish	Anti-Muslim
2001	1.83%	0.52%	7.18%	-5.95%	1617.86%
2002	-19.30%	-14.25%	-19.60%	-10.74%	-67.78%
2003	15.44%	2.49%	-11.25%	-0.43%	-3.87%
2004	-0.12%	7.18%	11.50%	2.91%	4.70%

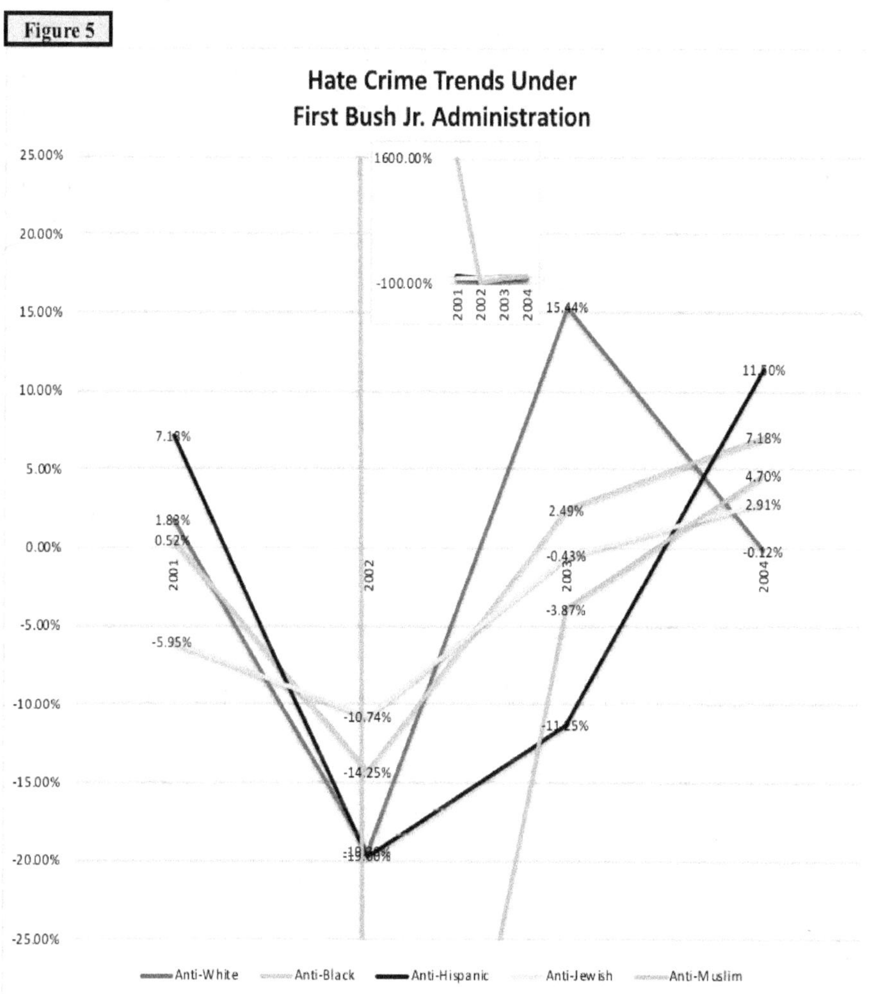

With Bush's first term, we can attribute much of the hate directed towards Muslims to the events of 9/11, but then in 2006 we see another rise of hate towards that group.

<table>
<tr><td colspan="6" align="center">Table 7</td></tr>
<tr><td colspan="6" align="center">Hate Crime Trends During Second Bush Administration</td></tr>
<tr><td>Year</td><td>Anti-White</td><td>Anti-Black</td><td>Anti-Hispanic</td><td>Anti-Jewish</td><td>Anti-Muslim</td></tr>
<tr><td>2004</td><td>-0.12%</td><td>7.18%</td><td>11.50%</td><td>2.91%</td><td>4.70%</td></tr>
<tr><td>2005</td><td>-0.12%</td><td>-3.70%</td><td>9.89%</td><td>-11.11%</td><td>-17.95%</td></tr>
<tr><td>2006</td><td>7.49%</td><td>0.38%</td><td>10.34%</td><td>14.03%</td><td>21.88%</td></tr>
<tr><td>2007</td><td>-15.84%</td><td>0.68%</td><td>3.30%</td><td>0.21%</td><td>-26.28%</td></tr>
<tr><td>2008</td><td>-4.41%</td><td>8.20%</td><td>-5.71%</td><td>4.54%</td><td>-8.70%</td></tr>
</table>

Figure 6

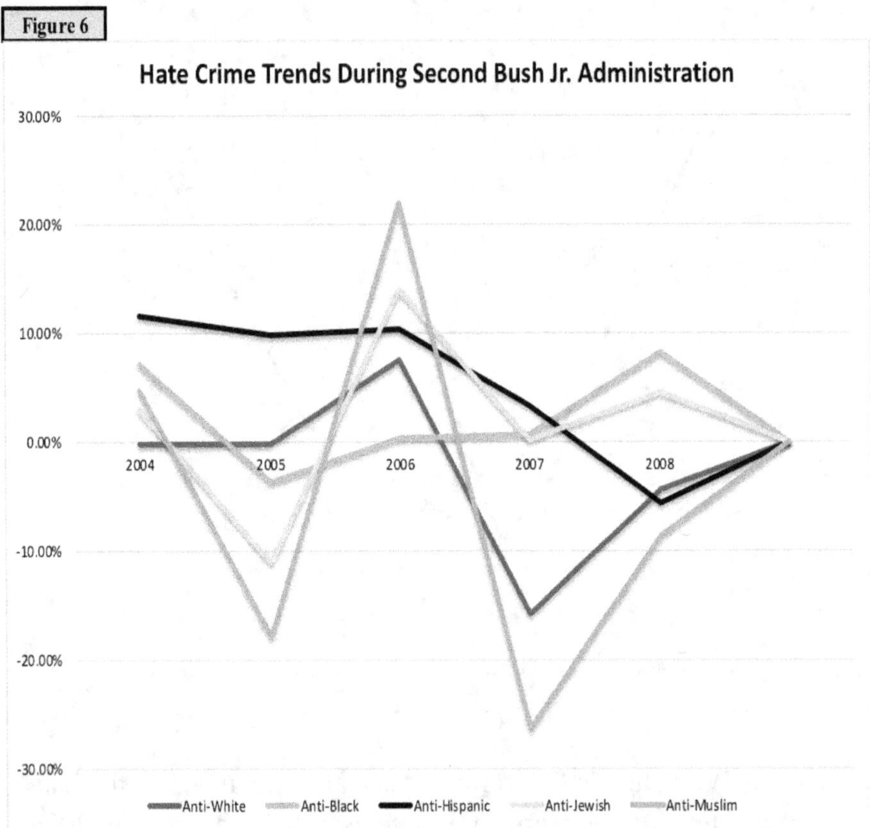

As President Obama took office, we saw a decrease in hate crime incidents throughout most of his first term. In 2010, there is a sharp rise in anti-Muslim incidents followed by a rise in anti-white incidents in 2012.

Table 8				
Hate Crime Trends During First Obama Administration				
Year	Anti-White	Anti-Black	Anti-Hispanic	Anti-Jewish	Anti-Muslim
2008	-4.41%	8.20%	-5.71%	4.54%	-8.70%
2009	-23.88%	-20.58%	-13.90%	-8.09%	1.90%
2010	5.50%	-3.63%	10.56%	-4.73%	49.53%
2011	-12.35%	-5.68%	-24.16%	-13.08%	-1.88%
2012	30.36%	-13.05%	-5.19%	-12.58%	-17.20%

Figure 7

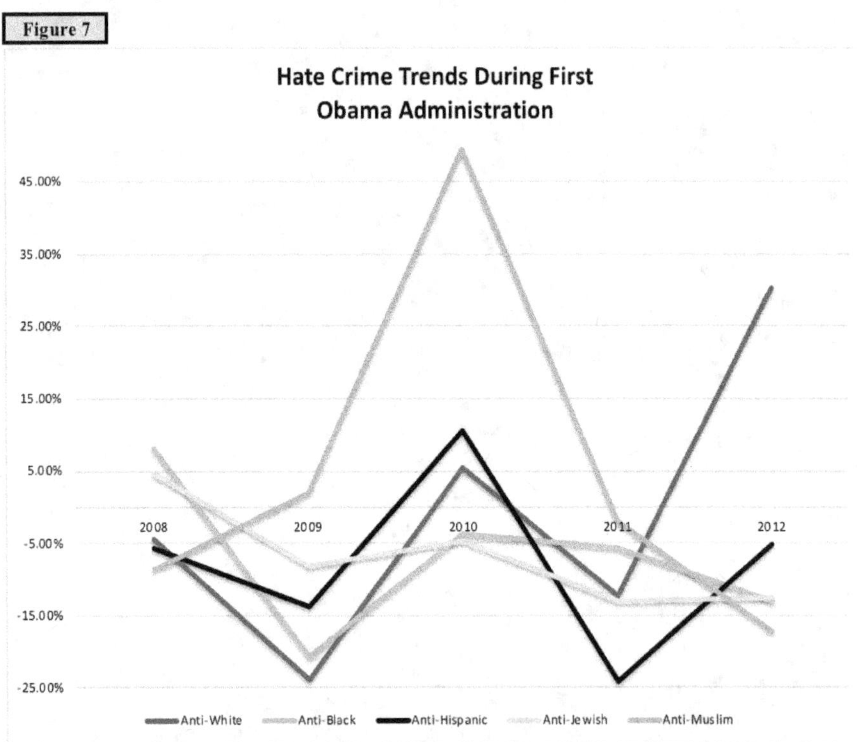

Otherwise, hate incidents seem to continue to decline during Obama's second term until 2015, the commencement year of Trump's campaign, where they begin to pick back up, particularly towards Muslims, Whites, and Hispanics.

Table 9					
Hate Crime Trends During Second Obama Administration					
Year	**Anti-White**	**Anti-Black**	**Anti-Hispanic**	**Anti-Jewish**	**Anti-Muslim**
2012	30.36%	-13.05%	-5.19%	-12.58%	-17.20%
2013	-0.61%	2.83%	-13.80%	-7.27%	3.85%
2014	-9.19%	-12.66%	-9.67%	-2.56%	14.07%
2015	3.37%	7.65%	0.00%	9.03%	66.88%
2016	23.98%	-0.34%	15.05%	3.01%	19.46%

Figure 8

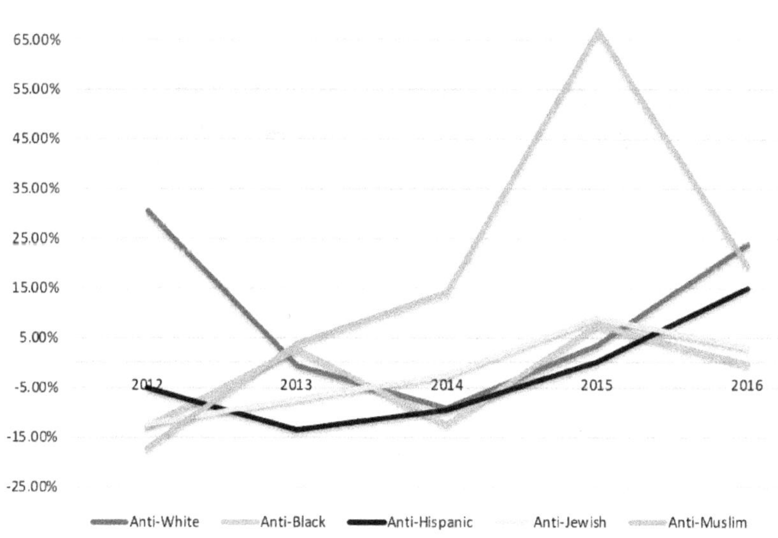

In 2016, Hispanics, a group targeted by Trump's immigration reform and deportation efforts, experienced a 15% increase in hate incidents.   An interesting and alarming increase of nearly 24% of reported hate incidents targeting white people also appears on our 2016 table and graph. This could either indicate a retaliation of hate by other groups towards whites, or a representation of increased hate towards minority groups who identify as white but are socially targeted for a different identifier such as ethnically being Arab. As in the case of Khalil Jabara, a White, Christian-Arab, murdered for being thought of as being Muslim.[115] It could also include hate crimes that involved white victims standing up to perpetrators attacking nonwhite targets. Either way, the rise of reports indicates the effects of a divisive campaign and hate-driven presidential leadership.

Table 10				
Hate Crime Trends Surrounding Trump Campaign				
Year	Anti-White	Anti-Black	Anti-Hispanic	Anti-Jewish	Anti-Muslim
2014	-9.19%	-12.66%	-9.67%	-2.56%	14.07%
2015	3.37%	7.65%	0.00%	9.03%	66.88%
2016	23.98%	-0.34%	15.05%	3.01%	19.46%

---

[115] D'Amours & Tahhan, 2016.

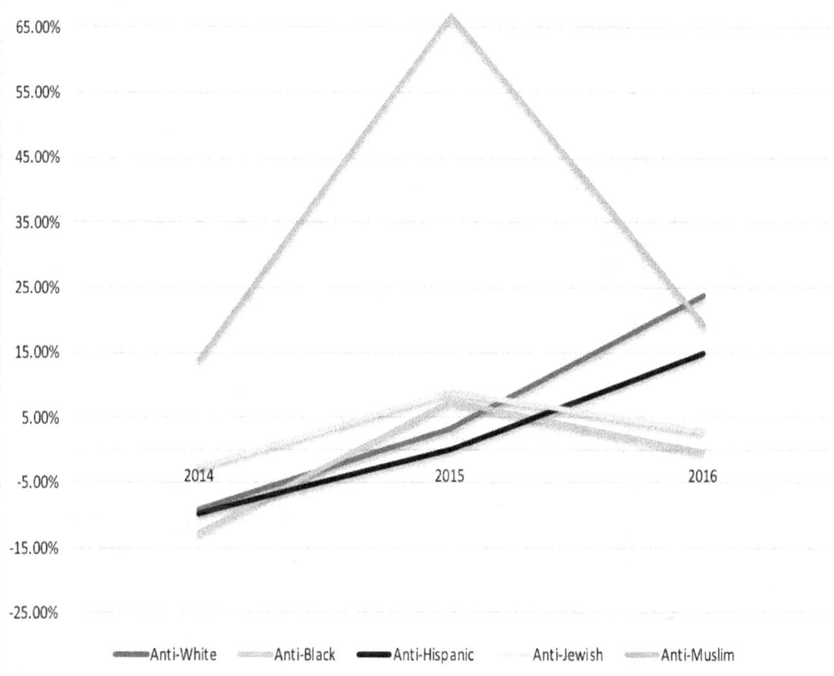

Tables 11, 12, and 13 calculate estimates of the populations of each minority that were directly targeted by hate crimes. These tables show that Jews, followed by Muslims, and Black Americans experienced the most hate crimes between 2014-2016.

Table 11			
Impact of Hate Crimes on Each Minority			
Year	**2014**		
Minority	**Most Recent Minority Population Estimates**	**Incidents**	**Percent of Minority Impacted**
Jews	5,700,000	609	0.010684%
Muslims	3,300,000	154	0.004667%
Black	45,672,250	1,621	0.003549%
Hispanic	58,000,000	299	0.000516%
White *	248,485,057	593	0.000239%
Female	164,148,777	23	0.000014%

*WHITE includes people having origins in Europe, the Middle East, or North Africa. It includes those of Irish, German, Italian, Lebanese, Arab, Moroccan, or Caucasian descent.

Table 12			
Impact of Hate Crimes on Each Minority			
Year	**2015**		
Minority	**Most Recent Minority Population Estimates**	**Incidents**	**Percent of Minority Impacted**
Jews	5,700,000	664	0.011649%
Muslims	3,300,000	257	0.007788%
Black	45,672,250	1,745	0.003821%
Hispanic	58,000,000	299	0.000516%
White *	248,485,057	613	0.000247%
Female	164,148,777	16	0.000010%

*WHITE includes people having origins in Europe, the Middle East, or North Africa. It includes those of Irish, German, Italian, Lebanese, Arab, Moroccan, or Caucasian descent.

Table 13			
Impact of Hate Crimes on Each Minority			
Year	**2016**		
Minority	**Most Recent Minority Population Estimates**	**Incidents**	**Percent of Minority Impacted**
Jews	5,700,000	684	0.012000%
Muslims	3,300,000	307	0.009303%
Black	45,672,250	1,739	0.003808%
Hispanic	58,000,000	344	0.000593%
White *	248,485,057	760	0.000306%
Female	164,148,777	24	0.000015%

*WHITE includes people having origins in Europe, the Middle East, or North Africa. It includes those of Irish, German, Italian, Lebanese, Arab, Moroccan, or Caucasian descent.

Table 14 sums up the effect of Trump's rhetoric. From 2014 to 2015, we see that Jews experienced an increase of about 9% in hate incidents while Muslims suffered nearly a 67% rise in hate. Black Americans also experienced a rise in hate by nearly 8%. With Trump's victorious election, Jewish hate slowed to a rise of 3%, while Muslim hate continued to increase by nearly 20%. Anti-Black/African incidents began to drop by 0.34% and we see a significant rise in anti-Hispanic hate from 0% to a rate of 15%. With Trump's anti-Mexican rhetoric and build-a-wall vision, it is evident that hate targeting this minority was perpetuated by Trump's anti-Hispanic political rhetoric. Although reports for anti-Female hate was limited to only a few years involved in this study, we see a significant rise of anti-female incidents by 50% from 2015-2016. Considering that there has never been a US president that has disparaged women openly in the way Trump has, we can conclude that his anti-female rhetoric has also emboldened criminals to act out in violence against this segment of American society as well.

Table 14		
Percents of Change		
Minority	**2014-2015 Percent**	**2015-2016 Percent**
Jews	9.03%	3.01%
Muslims	66.88%	19.46%
Black	7.65%	-0.34%
Hispanic or Latino	0.00%	15.05%
White *	3.37%	23.98%
Female	-30.43%	50.00%

Conclusion

Power without love is reckless and abusive, and love without power is sentimental and anemic. Power at its best is love implementing the demands of justice, and justice at its best is power correcting everything that stands against love.
–Martin Luther King Jr.

In *Peaceful Persuasion,* Ellen Gorsevki and Tom Hastings's discuss the power of language on minimizing or perpetuating hate. They elaborate on how the use of language can create systems of oppression and marginalize groups of people and how this occurred time and again throughout American history.

> Despite foundational ideals of freedom, United States history is rife with discrimination against certain groups of people or individuals who exhibit defining attributes. Prejudices and hatreds on the basis of religious affiliation, ethnicity, or sexual orientation, to name a few, have a long legacy that continues to haunt Americans today. Hate crimes are on the rise throughout the United States.[116]

By recognizing this reality alongside Trump's rhetoric and the reemergence of violence directed towards minorities

---

[116] Gorsevki & Hastings, 2004, 134.

during the 2016 campaign, it is evident that political language plays a significant role in the aggression marginalized communities face. The increased domestic violence was not the only result of an especially divisive and marginalizing campaign. Rhetoric often times transforms into policy if not acts of direct violence. Although structural violence is often invisible and therefore less addressed, it is a key perpetuator of direct violence and systems of oppression; it acts as the bedrock to a system of cultural and direct violence.

Trump's xenophobic rhetoric and intentions to enforce discriminatory policies specifically targeting minorities in the US strip these groups away of equality and set these marginalized communities even further behind. It then perpetuates acts of direct violence to be carried out towards these groups, adding a further layer of oppression and injustice towards the marginalized. Domestic issues targeting minority groups and immigrants directly impact America's global image and US international relations as well. The rise in anti-American sentiment puts Americans abroad at risk and negatively impacts interactions between the US and other nation states. The attempts at implementing structural methods of discrimination or implementing hate-inspired foreign policies such as the Muslim Ban or building a wall at the Mexican border further feed into white supremacist and violent nationalist ideologies that target minorities in acts of violence. This further divides the country and weakens the nation as a whole.

The importance of the change in the way that America is becoming reputed as an intolerant nation cannot be emphasized enough, primarily because it is one of the main propaganda techniques used by terrorist groups in recruiting followers. This research reveals how the Trump campaign feeds into that notion. America cannot afford to lend itself to aiding in this propaganda by stroking the fears of intolerance on both sides, therefore abetting in its own demise in the War on Terror.

Trump's rhetoric drastically undermines efforts to counter violent extremism. Extremism spreads at a faster rate when extremists are able to quote American leaders spewing out hate speech. Many people across the world are not introduced to Americans beyond what they are exposed to through the media. They are limited to only the image of our public officials. When they see the top-ranking American representative loudly spewing hate language directed at specific faiths or minority groups, it is highly unlikely that they are also seeing the domestic discourse refuting his speech made by a greater part of the American people. Many people abroad will likely adopt the impression that Americans are generally xenophobic people who hate certain religions or cultures, and are waging war against them simply for their faith or diverse ethnicities. This will cultivate a deep resentment for the American people all together, further fueling the hate that feeds extremist ideologies. Trump's campaign and presidential language is the type of discourse that creates these hate-inspired ideologies.

Anti-American sentiment has drastically increased over the past two decades. However, as our data demonstrate through a measure of hate crimes, Trump's influence has divided the nation even further through xenophobia and hate and perpetuated a bigoted image of the United States to the greater part of the world. Offensive and prejudice language by American political leaders sends the world the message that America is a racist, ethnocentric, and religiously intolerant nation. This image impacts American international relations with other governments and feeds into the propaganda used by extremist ideologies to recruit more members to their cause.

> The image of the United States has deteriorated significantly abroad since 2001, particularly in the Muslim world…The spread of anti-American feeling in the Islamic world is a serious problem for the United States. The growth of hostility to America in Muslim countries increases recruitment and support for extremism and terror.[117]

Trump's calls for building a wall and derogatory remarks about Mexicans have also fueled hate from our neighbors. Not only has his reckless language instigated a rise for hate towards Hispanics across the nation, it has also deteriorated American relations with Mexico.

Trump's leniency towards white supremacists and support for racist policies such as Stop-and-Frisk have also reignited a new blaze of racism that has long been battled in this country. His support for racist white supremacists and threats of violence towards others during his campaign has only proven to embolden and empower bigotry that has long been silenced in

---

[117] Robichaud & Goldbrenner, 2005.

the nation. This is not a good indication of a harmonious future for the stability of the country domestically, or abroad.

Racism and direct expressions of it are against the American value system, whether those values are enshrined into law or not. A large number of the American people were outraged at the audacity that anyone, let alone a presidential candidate, would have the insolence to instigate a new wave of hate that would target entire groups of people. Trump's efforts to explain himself resulted in him digging himself into a deeper hole with surrogates doubling in their efforts to defend him each and every time. Counterintuitively, his popularity continued to increase.

Violating America's spirit of respect and value for diversity, Trump continued with his divisive rhetoric on his path throughout the remainder of his campaign and eventually into his Presidency.

The current state of affairs has directly and immediately impacted our neighboring countries and even allies halfway across the globe. Aside from the effect on terrorism, the changing image of America from being the beacon of hope for immigrants from around the world to come and achieve "The American Dream" to one that favors nationalism and populism over globalization has had world altering effects from Brexit, Britain's choice to leave the European Union (EU), to worsening relations with our southern neighbor, Mexico, which helps the US in the War on Drugs and is a major contributor to our economy via being a consumer of US goods and products as a part of the Transpacific Partnership (TPP).

The UN's condemnation of Trump's declaration of Jerusalem as Israel's new capital also proved to earn the US severe disapproval from the greater international community. President Trump's statement initiated violence throughout the world and demonstrated a deep disregard for the decades of diplomatic efforts put forth regarding this extremely sensitive international issue.

It is my hope that this book has provided a better understanding of how the reckless and angry rhetoric of a political leader can have immediate and significant effects domestically as well as globally on a scale of issues. It is evident through the findings of our data that language can be extremely powerful. This truism suggests that people in power should only use powerful language to create positive change in the world. Political leaders are given a platform that billions across the world are not. They are granted authority with that and entrusted to lead the people in a way that will work towards greater peace and the well-being of all the people at large. President Donald Trump fails to realize the potential of his influence or the impact of his words on the world at large. His dialogue reveals much about his lack of understanding of the magnitude of his position as president of the United States and leader of the world. Communities, faith groups, and entire nations must cope with the effects of his words on their lives and work hard to repair the damage his words cause. Whether it be a surge in hate crimes or a rise in extremism, his choice of words in addressing our national and global issues is severely detrimental to the well-being of the millions and billions of people under his umbrella of leadership.

"The human capacity for hatred is terrifying in its volatility."[118] Throughout history we have observed hate-inspired leaders rally their people into monsters that have thoughtlessly persecuted millions of innocent lives, time and again, leaving us baffled at how we allowed such atrocities to occur within our human account. From Zedong to Hitler to Stalin,[119] political leaders were able to take the lives of tens of millions of people using the words they speak. Trump's hate-fueled rhetoric cannot be dismissed as merely empty words. Rather it must be identified based on its malicious tone as a call to all sorts of violence to be directed towards anyone that may fall short of the ethnically and religiously exclusive standards he and his followers deem to be American. This dangerous sentiment that he perpetuates in his leadership has demonstrated dire effects on American domestic stability as well as the United States' international relations with nations across the globe.

---

[118] Gopnik, 2017.

[119] Jones, 2014.

Tuning the Trumpet

...A good word is like a good tree, with its roots firm and its branches high in the sky, producing its fruit at all times...
Whereas a bad word is like a bad tree, uprooted and without stability.
-Quran 14:24-26

The words we choose create the life we experience and the world we create. The rhetoric we internalize wires our minds to view the world in a certain way which in-turn influences our interactions with others. We must be extremely selective with the words we choose as well as the narratives we allow to creep into our thoughts and become buried in the depths of our minds. We cannot allow negative rhetoric about different groups to influence our perceptions and in turn impact our interactions with those we don't instantly identify with. It is imperative to be proactive in dismantling negative messaging we are exposed to by challenging different forms of hate speech and negative stereotypes in order to better eliminate our own implicit biases.

Never in the history of humanity has it been found that hate and aggression leads to anything good. Violence breeds violence. Violent words inspire violent actions. They initiate the call for violent policies, provoke violent behavior, establish a culture of hostility, and create strife between people; limiting the potential for achieving the highest levels of success and harmony in any institution or country. Words of enmity have led to the subjugation, oppression, murders, and genocides of millions upon millions of innocent people. It is evident that hate fuels violence, always. It brings out barbaric traits in people.

So how do we achieve domestic and national security without resorting to the use of extremely aggressive and destructive language?

The answer to this question is honest individual introspection that inspires benevolence. Only by seeing others as being just as human as ourselves can we allow our differences to strengthen the framework of our country. Peace is something that starts from within, and when people achieve it within themselves, they will have the appropriate level of clarity to better address pertinent issues impacting their outside world. Love is often perceived as a weak attribute, while hate, rigidity, and aggression are oftentimes portrayed as traits of strength. However, reality proves otherwise. In societies that have relied on violence and divisiveness to establish authority and govern, faith in government declined, economies have suffered, crime rates increased, and in many cases, the state eventually fell apart. Our political approach needs to take into account the indisputable power rhetoric plays in the way the world works and how the language employed by political leaders has the potential of causing a state to crumble from within, if not making it vulnerable to the wrath of externals powers as well. Compassion is the remedy to heal and empower a wounded nation while language that inspires understanding and empathy is the medium in which it can be delivered.

We must keep in mind the role empathy plays as we move to become a more compassionate people in hopes of healing our wounded nation and understand the distinctness between the two. Chris Kukk's *The Compassionate Achiever*[120] distinguishes between empathy and compassion. Neurologically, with empathy, you feel what the other person is feeling. As mentioned earlier in this book, mirror neurons trigger the same neural pathways of pain in one's own brain upon connecting to the pain of another's. However, what we did not discuss was how it can potentially deplete us of emotional energy if we remain stuck there. Conversely, compassion, uses feelings of empathy to create feelings of care for another's struggles and moves you to take action in alleviating their pain. Empathy is crucial in paving the way to compassion. Compassion is simply empathy put into action. Furthermore, compassion induces the release of chemicals associated with that of love – oxytocin, dopamine, and serotonin – promoting brain stimulation and increasing mental capacity as well as cerebral potential for both giver and receiver. Words of love empower people to be the best versions of themselves. Through compassion (propelled by empathy) people can bring out the greatest of themselves and others, creating a greater America and better world.

Humanizing words allow people to realize their human potential, which in turn creates a stronger society and consequentially leads to higher levels of political dominance and global leadership. We must nurture our diversity and cultivate a culture of understanding if we truly wish to make America greater than it has ever been.

---

[120] Kukk, 2017.

Rather than fuel violence by trumpeting hate, it is imperative that political leaders use their words to extinguish injustice with compassion and foster a country that is sustained by the strength of a collectively healthy human spirit as opposed to a vicious self-imploding one.

Bibliography

Almasy, S., Hanna, J., Hartung, K., Sayers, D. & CNN. (August 13, 2017). "Virginia Governor to White Nationalists: 'Go Home ... Shame On You'." *CNN News*. Retrieved from http://www.cnn.com/2017/08/12/us/charlottesville-white-nationalists-rally/index.html

ACLU. (2008). *Discrimination against Muslim women.*

Al Wazni, A.B. (2015). *Muslim women in America and hijab: A study of empowerment, feminist identity, and body image. Social work 60 (4)*

Almasy, S., Yan, H., Lynch, J., Levenson, E., & CNN. (June 27, 2017). CNN. *No federal charges against officers in Alton Sterling death.* Retrieved from https://www.cnn.com/2017/05/03/us/alton-sterling-doj-death-investigation

Austin, A. (1997). *African Muslims in Antebellum America: transatlantic stories and spiritual struggles.* London: Routledge.

Banerji, R. (January 28, 2016). "In the dark: what is behind India's obsession with skin whitening?" *New Statesman America*. Retrieved from https://www.newstatesman.com/politics/feminism/2016/01/dark-what-behind-india-s-obsession-skin-whitening

Baugh, J. (2003). Linguistic profiling. In Makoni, Smitherman, Ball, and Spears (Ed.), Black linguistics. Language, society, and politics in Africa and the Americas (pp. 155-168). New York, NY: Routledge.

Berlinger, J., Valencia, N., & Almasy, S. (July 8, 2016.) CNN. Alton Sterling shooting: Homeless man made 911 call, source says. Retrieved from https://www.cnn.com/2016/07/07/us/baton-rouge-alton-sterling-shooting/index.html

Blanding, M. (December 18, 2018). Women Receive Harsher Punishment at Work Than Men. *Harvard Business School. Working Knowledge. Business Research for Business Leaders*. Retrieved from *https://hbswk.hbs.edu*

Bouie, Jamelle (November 7, 2016). "The Trump Campaign Is Ending as It Began: Bigoted as Hell." *Slate*. Retrieved from http://www.slate.com/articles/news_and_politics/politics/2016/11/trump_s_campaign_ends_as_it_began_with_bigotry_and_xenophobia.html

Brownstein, Ronald. (September 25, 2017). "The NFL, Charlottesville, and Trump's pattern of racial division." *CNN* Politics. Retrieved from http://www.cnn.com/2017/09/25/politics/trump-nfl-charlottesville/index.html

Bruce, H.A. (1912). *Woman in the Making of America*. Boston. The Colonial Press.

CairWebmaster. (February 13, 2018). CAIR and Walkup, Melodia file suit challenging Southwest Airlines' removal of Arabic-speaking passenger. *CAIR*. Retrieved from https://www.cair.com/cair_and_walkup_melodia_law_firm_file_suit_challenging_southwest_airlines_removal_of_arabic_speaking_passenger

Carter, S. & Sutch, R. (2006). *Resident Impacts of Immigration: Perspectives from America's Age of Mass Migration*. University of California.

Cavendish, J.C., Disha, I., and King, D. (2011, February). Historical events and spaces of hate: Hate crimes against Arabs and Muslims in post-9/11 America. *Social Problems, Vol. 58, No. 1*.

Chacar, H. (December 18, 2017). "Trump's Jerusalem announcement sparked deadly violence-from Israel." *The Intercept.* Retrieved from https://theintercept.com/2017/12/18/trump-jerusalem-israel-palestinian-protest/

CNN Wire. (May 30, 2017). "Portland Man Accused of Stabbing, Killing 2 Men Yells in Court: 'You Call it Terrorism, I Call It Patriotism'." *KTLA5 News*. Retrieved from http://ktla.com/2017/05/30/portland-man-accused-of-stabbing-killing-2-men-yells-in-court-you-call-it-terrorism-i-call-it-patriotism/

Cohen, Claire. (January 20, 2017) "Donald Trump Sexism Tracker: Every Offensive Comment in One Place." *The Telegraph*. Retrieved from http://www.telegraph.co.uk/women/politics/donald-trump-sexism-tracker-every-offensive-comment-in-one-place/

Collinson, S. & Diamond, J. (September 16, 2016). "Trump Finally Admits It: 'President Obama was born in the United States'." *CNN Politics*. Retrieved from: http://www.cnn.com/2016/09/15/politics/donald-trump-obama-birther-united-states/

Croft, J. (June 21, 2017.) CNN. *Philando Castile shooting: Dashcam video shows rapid event*. Retrieved from https://www.cnn.com/2017/06/20/us/philando-castile-shooting-dashcam/index.html

Curtin, P. (1972). *The Atlantic Slave Trade*. University of Wisconsin Press.

Curtis, E. E. (2009). *Muslims in America: A Short History*. Oxford: Oxford University Press.

D'Amours, J.K, & Tahhan, Z. (August 18, 2016). "Man in US killed in suspected 'anti-Arab hate crime'." *AlJazeera News*. Retrieved from http://www.aljazeera.com/news/2016/08/man-killed-suspected-anti-muslim-hate-crime-160816191517636.html

Dehlevi, Ghulam, New Age Islam. (2017). "Trump's Ban on Muslim Refugees: Counter-Terror Strategy or Politically Motivated Slugfest?." *Word for Peace*. Retrieved from http://www.wordforpeace.com/trumps-ban-on-muslim-refugees-counter-terror-strategy-or-politically-motivated-slugfest/

DelReal, J. (June 16, 2015). "Donald Trump announces presidential bid." *Washington Post*. Retrieved from https://www.washingtonpost.com/news/post-politics/wp/2015/06/16/donald-trump-to-announce-his-presidential-plans-today/?utm_term=.d2cf20eaca11

Derosa, P. (2016, May). "Was America built by slaves?" *The American Interest, 11*, 1-8. Retrieved from http://search.proquest.com.ezp-prod1.hul.harvard.edu/docview/1792734793?accountid=11311

Desilver, Drew & Masci, David. (January 31, 2017). "World's Muslim populations more widespread than you might think." *Pew Research Center*. Retrieved from www.pewresearch.org/fact-tank/2017/01/31/worlds-muslim-population-more-widespread-than-you-might-think/

Diouf, S. A.(2013). Servants of Allah: African Muslims Enslaved in the Americas, 15th Anniversary Edition. New York: NYU Press. Retrieved January 27, 2018, from Project MUSE database.

Dougherty, Kevin. (January 31, 2017). "Quebec Mosque shooting suspect was a fan of Donald Trump and Marine le Pen." *The Independent US*. Retrieved from http://www.independent.co.uk/news/world/americas/quebec-city-mosque-shooting-latest-alexandre-bissonnette-donald-trump-marine-le-pen-facebook-social-a7554451.html

Eagleton Institute of Politics. Rutgers. (2017). "Women in the U.S Congress 2017." *Center for American Women and Politics*. Retrieved from http://www.cawp.rutgers.edu/women-us-congress-2017

Elkins, A. (May 9, 2015). "The Origins of Stop-and-Frisk." *Jacobin*. Retrieved from https://www.jacobinmag.com/2015/05/stop-and-frisk-dragnet-ferguson-baltimore/

Fawcett, M. G. (1912). *Women's Suffrage; A Short History of a Great Movement*. London; Edinburgh: T. C. & E. C. Jack. Retrieved from

http://tinyurl.galegroup.com.ezp-
prod1.hul.harvard.edu/tinyurl/5RTD49

Fish, Steven. (2011). *Are Muslims Distinctive? A Look at the Evidence.*
Oxford University Press.

Fisher, M. (August 16, 2017). Washington Post. *Trump and race: Decades of
fueling divisions.* Retrieved from
https://www.washingtonpost.com/politics/trump-and-race-decades-
of-fueling-divisions/2017/08/16/5fb3cd7c-8296-11e7-b359-
15a3617c767b_story.html?utm_term=.fad53459af33

Galtung, J. (1969). "Violence, Peace, and Peace Research." *Journal of Peace
Research. Vol 6, No. 3.* Retrieved from http://www2.kobe-
u.ac.jp/~alexroni/IPD%202015%20readings/IPD%202015_2/Galtun
g_Violence,%20Peace,%20and%20Peace%20Research.pdf

Gaouette, N. (December 21, 2017). "Despite Haley threat, UN votes to
condemn Trump's Jerusalem decision." *CNN Politics.* Retrieved
from http://www.cnn.com/2017/12/21/politics/haley-un-
jerusalem/index.html

Gopnik, Adam. (February 20, 2017). "Trump's radical anti-Americanism."
The New Yorker. Retrieved from
http://www.newyorker.com/magazine/2017/02/13/trumps-radical-
anti-americanism

Gorsevski, E. W. & Hastings, T. H. (2004). *Peaceful Persuasion: The
Geopolitics of Nonviolent Rhetoric.* Retrieved from
https://muse.jhu.edu/

Guterl, M. (2008). "Latino Americans." *In Oxford Encyclopedia of the
Modern World. : Oxford University Press.* Retrieved from
http://www.oxfordreference.com.ezp-
prod1.hul.harvard.edu/view/10.1093/acref/9780195176322.001.000
1/acref-9780195176322-e-885.

Hirschman, C., & Mogford, E. (2009). "Immigration and the American
Industrial Revolution From 1880 to 1920." *Social Science Research,
38*(4), 897–920. http://doi.org/10.1016/j.ssresearch.2009.04.001

Hirschman, C., Kasinitz, P., & Dewind, J. (1999). *The Handbook of
International Migration: The American Experience.* Russell Sage
Foundation. Retrieved from https://muse.jhu.edu/.

Holan, A. (August 26, 2010). "Why do so many people think Obama is
Muslim?" *Politifact.* Retrieved from
http://www.politifact.com/truth-o-meter/article/2010/aug/26/why-
do-so-many-people-think-obama-muslim/

Hutchinson, E. O. (October 8, 2017). Huffington Post. *Trump race baits with The Central Park Five case—Yet again.* Retrieved from https://www.huffingtonpost.com/earl-ofari-hutchinson/trump-race-baits-with-the_b_12392112.html

Institute for Women's Policy Research. (2016). *Undervalued and Underpaid in America: Women in Low-Wage, Female-Dominated Jobs.* Retrieved from https://iwpr.org/wp-content/uploads/wpallimport/files/iwpr-export/publications/D508%20Undervalued%20and%20Underpaid.pdf

Jewish Virtual Library. (2017). "Vital Statistics: Jewish Population in the United States, by State (1899 - Present)." *American-Israeli Cooperative Enterprise.* Retrieved from https://www.jewishvirtuallibrary.org/jewish-population-in-the-united-states-by-state

Jones, Nigel. (October 7, 2014). "From Stalin to Hitler, the most murderous regimes in the world." *Mail Online.* Retrieved from http://www.dailymail.co.uk/home/moslive/article-2091670/Hitler-Stalin-The-murderous-regimes-world.html

Kearns, E.M., Betus, A. & Lemieux, A. (2017). "Why Do Some Terrorist Attacks Receive More Media Attention Than Others?" *Justice Quarterly.* Retrieved from https://www.erinmkearns.com/uploads/2/4/5/5/24559611/kearnsbetuslemieux.2018.jq.mediacoverageterrorism.pdf

Kukk, C. (2017). *The compassionate achiever: How Helping Others Fuel Success.* New York, NY: Harper Collins Publisher

Lakoff, G. (September 8, 2017). "Why hate speech is not free speech." Retrieved from https://georgelakoff.com/2017/09/08/why-hate-speech-is-not-free-speech/

Landler, M. (December 6, 2017). "Trump recognizes Jerusalem as Israel's capital and orders U.S. embassy move." *The New York Times.* Retrieved from https://www.nytimes.com/2017/12/06/world/middleeast/trump-jerusalem-israel-capital.html

Laughland, O. (February 17, 2016). The Guardian. *Donald Trump and the Central Park Five: the racially charged rise of a demagogue.* Retrieved from https://www.theguardian.com/us-news/2016/feb/17/central-park-five-donald-trump-jogger-rape-case-new-york

Lee, J. (May 23, 2017). "WH: Trump was 'exhausted' when he said 'Islamic extremism'." *CNN*. Retrieved from: http://www.cnn.com/2017/05/22/politics/trump-islamic-islamist/

Lichtblau, E. (November 14, 2016) "US Hate Crimes Surge 6%, Fueled by Attacks on Muslims." *The New York Times*. Retrieved from: https://www.nytimes.com/2016/11/15/us/politics/fbi-hate-crimes-muslims.html?_r=1

Lichtblau. E. (September 17, 2016). Hate crimes against American Muslims most since post 9/11 era. *The New York Times*. Retrieved from http://www.nytimes.com/2016/09/18/us/politics/hate-crimes-american-muslims- rise.html?partner=rss&emc=rss.

Lopez, G. (November 14, 2018). "There are huge racial disparities in how US police use force." *VOX*. Retrieved from https://www.vox.com/identities/2016/8/13/17938186/police-shootings-killings-racism-racial-disparities

Luqman, M. (2018). *The Trump Effect: Impacts of Political Rhetoric on Minorities and America's Image*. (Master's thesis, Cambridge, MA/ Harvard University, 2018) (pp. 1-78). Cambridge: Harvard University.

McCrackan, E. (1905). *The Woman of America*. New York: Macmillan. Retrieved from http://tinyurl.galegroup.com.ezp-prod1.hul.harvard.edu/tinyurl/5RAty2

McIntosh, P. (1988). "White Privilege and Male Privilege: A Personal Account of Coming to See Correspondences Through Work in Women's Studies" Wellesley: Center for Research on Women.

McIntosh, P. (1990). "White Privilege: Unpacking the Invisible Knapsack." Philadelphia, PA: Independent School.

Miah, M. (2017, Mar). "Leadership role of African Americans: Make Trump's America ungovernable." *Against the Current, 32*, 2-3. Retrieved from http://search.proquest.com.ezp-prod1.hul.harvard.edu/docview/1877374586?accountid=11311

Mohamed, B. (January 6, 2016). "A New Estimate of the US Muslim Population." *Pew Research Center*. Retrieved from http://www.pewresearch.org/fact-tank/2016/01/06/a-new-estimate-of-the-u-s-muslim-population/

Moshtaghian, A., Wu, H., and Cullinane, S., (March 6, 2017). "Sikh man's shooting in Washington investigated as hate crime." *CNN*. Retrieved from http://edition.cnn.com/2017/03/05/us/washington-sikh-shooting/index.html

Murrow, G., and Murrow, R. (June 8, 2015). "A hypothetical neurological association between dehumanization and human rights abuses." *Journal of Law and the Biosciences.*

NAACP. (2018). "Criminal justice fact sheet." Retrieved from https://www.naacp.org/criminal-justice-fact-sheet/

Nossel, S. (August 14, 2017). "The Problem with Making Hate Speech Illegal." *Foreign Policy.* Retrieved from http://foreignpolicy.com/2017/08/14/the-problem-with-making-hate-speech-illegal-trump-charlottesville-virginia-nazi-white-nationalist-supremacist/

O'Connor, Lydia & Marans, Daniel. (February 29, 2016) "Here Are 13 Examples of Donald Trump Being Racist." *The Huffington Post.* Retrieved from: http://www.huffingtonpost.com/entry/donald-trump-racist-examples_us_56d47177e4b03260bf777e83

Peters, M. C. (1905). *The Jews in America: A Short Story of Their Part in the Building of the Republic: Commemorating the Two Hundred and Fiftieth Anniversary of Their Settlement.* (pp. 1-164).

Pew Research Center. (April 2, 2015). "The Future of World Religions: Population Growth Projections, 2010-2050." *Pew Research Center.* Retrieved from http://www.pewforum.org/2015/04/02/religious-projections-2010-2050/

Robichaud, Carol & Goldbrenner, Rachel. (June 30, 2005). "Anti-Americanism and Violence." *Princeton Project on National Security.* Retrieved from https://www.princeton.edu/~ppns/papers/robichaudAAwithappend.pdf

Robson, B. (2006). "Running Man." *City Pages.* Retrieved from http://www.citypages.com/news/running-man-6689842

Rogers, J. A. (2014). "Africa's Gift to America: The Afro-American in the Making and Saving of the United States." *Middletown: Wesleyan University Press.* Retrieved October 25, 2017, from Project MUSE database.

Roginsky, A. & Tsesis. (April 3, 2016). "Hate speech, volition, and neurology." *Journal of Law and the Biosciences.*

SAALT. (2017). "Power, Pain, Potential." *South Asian Americans at the Forefront of Growth and Hate in the 2016 Election Cycle.*

Sarlin, B. (October 7, 2016). NBC News. *Donald Trump Says Central Park Five Are Guilty, Despite DNA Evidence.* Retrieved from https://www.nbcnews.com/politics/2016-election/donald-trump-says-central-park-five-are-guilty-despite-dna-n661941

Schwartz, B. (2015). *The Emancipation Proclamation: Lincoln's Many Second Thoughts.* Department of Sociology, University of Georgia.

Senanayake, D. (July 31, 2018). "When Fair isn't fair and Lovely isn't lovely in Sri Lanka." *DJED Press.* Retrieved from https://djedpress.com/2018/07/31/unfairandlovely-in-sri-lanka/

Sidbury, J. (2007). *In Becoming African in America: Race and Nation in the Early Black Atlantic, 1760-1830.*: Oxford University Press.

Smith, B. (2016, Nov). "Four more things for African Americans to consider in Trump's America." *Tri - State Defender* Retrieved from http://search.proquest.com.ezp-prod1.hul.harvard.edu/docview/1860258772?accountid=11311

Smith, J. (2010). *Islam in America.* Colombia University Press.

Smith, K. (March 11, 2017). "Trump's new Muslim ban already faces push back." *Green Left Weekly.* Retrieved from https://www.greenleft.org.au/content/trump%E2%80%99s-new-muslim-ban-already-faces-push-back

Smith, W., Allen, W., & Danley, L. (December 2007). "Assume the Position . . . You Fit the Description. Psychosocial Experiences and Racial Battle Fatigue Among African American Male College Students." *American Behavioral Scientist.*

Spellberg, D. (2013). *Thomas Jefferson's Qur'an: Islam and the Founders.* Alfred A. Knopf New York.

Stack, L. (April 17, 2016). College student is removed from flight after speaking Arabic on planc. The New York Times. Retrieved from https://www.nytimes.com/2016/04/17/us/student-speaking-arabic-removed-southwest-airlines-plane.html

Sundance Selects, WETA, Florentine Films, PBS, The Central Park Five Film Project, F.M. (Producers), & Burns, K., Burns, S., McMahon, D., F.M. (Directors). (2012). *The Central Park Five.* (Video filc). Retrieved from https://www.amazon.com/Ken-Burns-Central-Park-Five/dp/B00BYEVUWI

Talbot, M. (Jun 22, 2015). The story of a hate crime. The New Yorker. Retrieved from http://search.proquest.com.ezp-prod1.hul.harvard.edu/docview/1694960265?accountid=11311.

Tatum, S. & CNN. (September 23, 2017). "Trump: NFL owners should fire players who protest the national anthem." *CNN Politics.* Retrieved from http://www.cnn.com/2017/09/22/politics/donald-trump-alabama-nfl/index.html

Timmermann, W. (December 2008). "Counteracting hate speech as a way of preventing genocidal violence." *Genocide Studies and Prevention*

Volume 3, Issue 3. P. 353-374. Retrieved from
https://scholarcommons.usf.edu/cgi/viewcontent.cgi?referer=https://
www.google.com/&httpsredir=1&article=1164&context=gsp

The Intraracial Colorism Project. (2018). "Colorism defined." *The Intraracial
Colorism Project, Inc.* Retrieved from http://colorismproject.com

United Nations Office of High Commissioner of Human Rights. (July, 6,
2018). *USA / People of African descent: UN expert group condemns
recent killings.* Retrieved from
https://www.ohchr.org/EN/NewsEvents/Pages/DisplayNews.aspx?N
ewsID=20248&LangID=E

United States District Court For the Eastern District of New York, (1975).
Washington Post. Complaint for injunction pursuant to Fair Housing
Ac of 1968, 42 U.S.C. 3601. Retrieved from
https://www.washingtonpost.com/wp-stat/graphics/politics/trump-
archive/docs/us-v-trump-case-via-national-archives-foia.pdf

U.S. Census Bureau (November 23, 2015). *Statistical Abstract of the United
States: 2012.* Retrieved from
https://www.census.gov/library/publications/2011/compendia/statab/
131ed/population.html

US Census Bureau. (March 16, 2016). *FFF: Women's History Month: March
2016.* Retrieved from https://www.census.gov/newsroom/facts-for-
features/2016/cb16-ff03.html

US Congress. (April 2016). *Gender pay inequality. Consequences for
women, families, and the economy.* Retrieved from
https://www.jec.senate.gov/public/_cache/files/0779dc2f-4a4e-
4386-b847-9ae919735acc/gender-pay-inequality----us-congress-
joint-economic-committee.pdf

U.S. Department of Health and Human Services. (2013). *Results from the
2013 National Survey on Drug Use and Health: Summary of
National Findings.* Retrieved from
https://www.samhsa.gov/data/sites/default/files/NSDUHresultsPDF
WHTML2013/Web/NSDUHresults2013.pdf

US Department of Justice. (2000-2015). *Hate Crime Statistics 2000-2015.
(Federal Bureau of Investigation Uniform Crime Reporting).*
Washington, DC. US Government Printing Office.

US Department of Justice. (2014). *Hate Crime Statistics 2014 (Federal
Bureau of Investigation Uniform Crime Reporting).* Washington,
DC. US Government Printing Office.

US Department of Justice. (2016). *Hate Crime Statistics 2016 (Federal Bureau of Investigation Uniform Crime Reporting)*. Washington, DC. US Government Printing Office.

US Department of Justice. (2005). *Terrorism 2002/2005 (Federal Bureau of Investigation)*. Retrieved from https://www.fbi.gov/stats-services/publications/terrorism-2002-2005

US Government Accountability Office. (April 2017). *Countering Violent Extremism*. Retrieved from https://www.gao.gov/assets/690/683984.pdf

Varigny, C. V. C. D. (1895). "The Women of the United States." New York: *Dodd, Mead and Co.* Retrieved from http://tinyurl.galegroup.com.ezp-prod1.hul.harvard.edu/tinyurl/5RAtx4

Voloch, E. (June 19, 2017). "Supreme Court unanimously reaffirms: There is no 'hate speech' exception to the First Amendment." *The Washington Post*. Retrieved from https://www.washingtonpost.com/news/volokh-conspiracy/wp/2017/06/19/supreme-court-unanimously-reaffirms-there-is-no-hate-speech-exception-to-the-first-amendment/?utm_term=.a0c21d798452

Washington Post Staffer. (June 16, 2015). "Donald Trump announces a presidential Bid." *Washington Post*. Retrieved from https://www.washingtonpost.com/news/post-politics/wp/2015/06/16/full-text-donald-trump-announces-a-presidential-bid/?utm_term=.6a6011ca18bd

Webb, S. (July 20, 2015). "Colorism is a symptom and system of oppression?" *Colorism Healing*. Retrieved from https://colorismhealing.org/symptom-system/

Wiernik, P. (1912). "History of the Jews in America: from the period of the discovery of the New World to the present time." New York: *Jewish Press Pub. Co.* Retrieved from http://nrs.harvard.edu/urn-3:FHCL:881267

Williams, V. V. (2011). "Brothers of the trade: Intersections of racial framing and identity processes upon African-Americans and African immigrants in America—ancestral kinsmen of the American slave trade." *ProQuest Dissertations & Theses Global*. Retrieved from http://search.proquest.com.ezp-prod1.hul.harvard.edu/docview/885230751?accountid=11311

Winter, J. (August 14, 2017). "FBI and DHS Warned of Growing Threat

From White Supremacists Months Ago." *Foreign Policy*. Retrieved from https://foreignpolicy.com/2017/08/14/fbi-and-dhs-warned-of-growing-threat-from-white-supremacists-months-ago/

Footnotes

[1]Timmerman, 2008.

[2]Volokh, 2017.

[3]Murrow & Murrow, 2015.

[4]Roginsky & Tsesis, 2016.

[5]Lakoff, 2017.

[6]Roginsky & Tsesis, 2016.

[7]Holan, 2010.

[8]DelReal, 2015.

[9]O'Connor & Marans, February 29, 2016.

[10]Black Lives Matter: the name of a movement founded in 2013 in response to the disparity in value for black lives in the United States and to bring awareness to police brutality targeting black men across the nation.

[11]O'Connor & Marans, February 29, 2016.

[12]Dougherty, January 31, 2017.

[13]Moshtaghian, Wu, & Cullinane, March 6, 2017.

[14]CNN Wire, May 30, 2017.

[15]Hirschman, Kasinitz, & Dewind, 1999, 1.

[16]Derosa, 2016.

[17]Schwartz, 2015.

[18]Carter & Sutch, 2006, 5.

[19]Carter & Sutch, 2006, 5.

[20]Hirschman, Kasinitz, & Dewind, 1999, 1.

[21]Hirschman, Kasinitz, & Dewind, 1999, 1.

[22]Hirschman, Kasinitz, & Dewind, 1999, 8.

[23]US Census, 2010.

[24]Curtin, 1972, 5.

[25]Elkins, 2015.

[26]People [person] of color: a term used to identify those who are not of European heritage.

[27]Lopez, November 14, 2018.

[28]United Nations Office of High Commissioner of Human Rights, July, 6, 2018.

[29]Croft, CNN, June 21, 2017.

[30]Almasy, Yan, Lynch, & Levenson, CNN, June 27, 2017. Berlinger, Valencia, & Almasy, CNN, July 8, 2016.

[31]Lopez, November 14, 2018 & U.S. Department of Health and Human Services, 2013.

[32]Lopez, November 14, 2018.

[33]NAACP, 2018.

[34]Sundance Selects, WETA, Florentine Films, PBS, The Central Park Five Film Project, 2012.

[35]Fisher, August 16, 2017. Hutchinson, October 8, 2017. Laughland, February 17, 2016. Sarlin, October 7, 2016.

[36]United States District Court For the Eastern District of New York, 1975.

[37]Collinson & Diamond, September 16, 2016.

[38]Almasy, S., Hanna, J., Hartung, K., Sayers, D. & CNN, August 13, 2017.

[39]Tatum, September 23, 2017.

[40]Brownstein, September 25, 2017.

[41]US Census, 2010.

[42]Gutrel, 2008.

[43]Washington Post Staffer. June 16, 2015.

[44]O'Connor & Marans, February 29, 2016.

[45]Washington Post Staffer, June 16, 2015.

[46]Annual Estimates of the Resident Population for Selected Age Groups by Sex for the United States, States, Counties and Puerto Rico Commonwealth and Municipios: April 1, 2010 to July 1, 2016 Source: U.S. Census Bureau, Population Division Release Date: June 2017.

[47]Blanding, December 18, 2018.

[48]Institute for Women's Policy Research, 2016.

[49]Institute for Women's Policy Research, 2016.

[50]United States Congress, 2016.

[51]Institute for Women's Policy Research, 2016.

[52]US Census, 2016.

[53]Institute for Women's Policy Research, 2016.

[54]Fawcett, 1912, 8.

[55]Center for American Women and Politics, 2017.

[56]Cohen, January 20, 2017.

[57]Peters, 1905.

[58]Pew Research Center, 2015 & Jewish Virtual Library, 2017.

[59]Aslan & Tapper, 2011.

[60]Collinson & Diamond, September 16, 2016.

[61]Landler, 2017.

[62]Chacar, 2017 & Gaouette, 2017.

[63]Robson, 2006.

[64]Curtis, 2009, 4.

[65]Curtis, 2009, 5.

[66]Curtin, 1972.

[67]Austin, 1997 & Diouf, 2013.

[68]Curtis, 2009, 50.

[69]Pew Research Center, 2015.

[70]Smith, 2010, Chapter 3.

[71]Smith, 2010, Chapter 3.

[72]Smith, 2010, Chapter 3.

[73]Lee, May 23, 2017.

[74]SAALT, 2017, 3.

[75]Desilver & Masci, 2017.

[76]Pew Research Center, 2015.

[77]SAALT, 2017, 3.

[78]SAALT, 2017, 16.

[79]Al Wazni, 2015, 326.

[80]Lichtblau, September 17, 2016.

[81]Al Wazni, 2015, 326.

[82]Talbot, June 22, 2015.

[83]Talbot, June 22, 2015.

[84]Talbot, June 22, 2015.

[85]Talbot, June 22, 2015.

[86]Lichtblau, September 17, 2016.

[87]ACLU, 2008.

[88]US Department of Justice, 2015.

[89]Government Accountability Office, 2017.

[90]Kearns, Betus, & Lemieux, 2017.

[91]US Department of Justice, 2005.

[92]US Department of Justice, 2005.

93Winter, 2017.

94Racial Battle Fatigue: the emotional, physical, and psychological toll a person of color experiences due to constant discrimination, micro-aggressions, and stereotype threat.

95Smith, 2007.

96McIntosh, 1988.

97Banerji, January 28, 2016 & Senanayake, July 31, 2018.

98Banerji, January 28, 2016 & Senanayake, July 31, 2018.

99Webb, July 20, 2015.

100Baugh, 2003.

101Baugh, 2003.

102Stack, 2016 & CAIR Webmaster 2018.

103Bouie, 2016.

104US Department of Justice, 2015.

105US Department of Justice, 2017.

106Calculations are estimates based on data available.

107"White: A person having origins in any of the original peoples of Europe, the Middle East, or North Africa. It includes people who indicate their race as "White" or report entries such as Irish, German, Italian, Lebanese, Arab, Moroccan, or Caucasian." (US Census, 2014).

108US Census, 2014.

109US Census, 2014.

110Pew Research Center, 2017.

111Pew Research Center, 2013.

112US Census, 2016.

113US Census, 2014.

114Totals may not add up to exactly one hundred percent.

115D'Amours & Tahhan, 2016.

116Gorsevki & Hastings, 2004, 134.

117Robichaud & Goldbrenner, 2005.

118Gopnik, 2017.

119Jones, 2014.

120Kukk, 2017.

www.ingramcontent.com/pod-product-compliance
Lightning Source LLC
Chambersburg PA
CBHW070124260726

48658CB00001B/248